What People Say About *Chicken Soup for the Teenage Soul Journal* . . .

"This is so much more than a journal. I always think of a journal as blank pages. This is filled with great quotes, great poems, great questions and great cartoons. I love it!"

Kate, 16

"This will be my most valuable possession once I have filled it with my answers and my stories. I love that it has places for my friends and my boyfriend to write stuff to me."

Kirsten, 16

"I always try to write in journals but I never do because I get bored. I know I will finish this one because it helps every step of the way. I'm so excited to start writing in it."

Toby, 13

"What a great idea! When I am finished writing in this journal I will have my own *Chicken Soup* book."

Erica, 14

"Writing about what we are feeling is so important for teenagers. This journal is so great because it helps us think of what things we need to write about. I think this book is brilliant."

Jason, 18

"Finally somebody understands what teenagers like and need! This is the perfect journal/book for teenagers."

Susie, 17

"I bought this journal for my fourteen-year-old daughter and she loves it. I keep finding her in her room writing in it. It makes me happy that she has a book that is helping her to think about her life and her values."

Veronica, mother

CHICKEN SOUP
FOR THE
TEENAGE SOUL
Journal

Jack Canfield
Mark Victor Hansen
Kimberly Kirberger

Health Communications, Inc.
Deerfield Beach, Florida

www.hci-online.com
www.chickensoup.com
www.teenagechickensoup.com

We would like to acknowledge the many publishers and individuals who granted us permission to reprint the cited material. (Note: The stories that were penned anonymously, that are in the public domain, or that were written by Jack Canfield, Mark Victor Hansen or Kimberly Kirberger are not included in this listing.)

I AM . . . Reprinted by permission of Khendi White. ©1998 Khendi White.

Teenager. Reprinted by permission of Jamie Newland. ©1996 Jamie Newland.

Myself and *You Tell On Yourself.* Reprinted by permission of *Peer Counsellor Workbook.* ©1988 *Peer Counsellor Workbook.*

I AM. Reprinted by permission of Kathryn Mockett. ©1998 Kathryn, Mockett.

Let Me Lean On You. Reprinted by permission of Lissa Barker and Donna Barker. ©1996 Lissa Barker.

I AM YOUR CHILD. Denise Marigold. Reprinted by permission of Denise Marigold. ©1998 Denise Marigold.

(Continued on page 340)

Library of Congress Cataloging-in-Publication Data

Canfield, Jack, date.
    Chicken soup for the teenage soul: journal / Jack Canfield, Mark Victor Hansen, Kimberly Kirberger.
      p. cm.
    ISBN 1-55874-637-4 (trade paper)
    1. Teenagers—Conduct of life.—Problems, exercises, etc.
    I. Hansen, Mark Victor, date. II. Kirberger, Kimberly, date. III. Title.
    BJ1661.C5C33 1998
    158.1'2—dc21   98-36018
                                             CIP

Publisher: Health Communications, Inc.
               3201 S.W. 15th Street
               Deerfield Beach, FL 33442-8190

R-09-01

Cover artwork by Robbin O'Neill
Inside graphics by Robbin O'Neill
Cover redesign by Andrea Perrine Brower

With love we dedicate this journal to
Jesse, Christopher, Elisabeth, Melanie, Chelsea, Adam,
Joey, Jessie, Juliana, Hannah, Hana, Lisa, Bree, Ashley,
Michael, Lyndsey, Lyle, Marissa, Daniel,
Katrina, Tommy, Lisa R., Kelly, Lia, Blake, Jamie,
Caitlin, Hayley, Lily, Taycora and
every other teen we have had the pleasure
of knowing—you are our inspiration.

We also dedicate this journal to all the teenagers who
shared their stories and poems with us. We were
touched by each and every one of them.

Finally, we dedicate this book to God,
from whom all blessings flow.

Contents

Acknowledgments

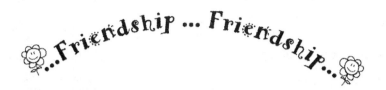

This journal was such an incredible challenge and joy to write. We stepped into the hearts and minds of teenagers in order to give you a book that would offer insight and guidance during these challenging years. It was because of the help, support and love from the following people that this was possible.

First and foremost we want to thank our parents, Ellen Taylor and Fred Angelis, and Paul and Una Hansen, for raising us and putting up with us when we were teenagers.

A big thank-you to Kimberly's husband, John, Mark's wife, Patty and Jack's wife, Georgia, for the love and support they give us.

To our beloved children: Jesse, Christopher, Kyle, Oran, Elisabeth and Melanie, for their daily doses of inspiration and for giving us such wonderful purpose.

To Mitch Claspy, for his brilliance, patience and commitment. Words cannot express our gratitude.

To Robbin O'Neill, for doing all the graphics and for being such a pleasure to work with on this project. Robbin, you are a true artist.

To Jessie Braun, our favorite teenager, for brightening Kimberly's days with her support and for her crystal-clear feedback on all the teenage projects.

To Laurie Hanna, Brigette English and Kelly Harrington, for their work on the book and with the Teen Letter Project. We thank you all.

To Kim Foley, for being such a good friend to Kimberly.

To Patty Aubery, Heather McNamara and Nancy Mitchell for all they do and for their never-ending support.

To Leslie Forbes, Theresa Esparza, Ro Miller, Veronica Romero, Robin Yerian and Lisa Williams for handling so many things in Jack's and Mark's offices.

To Barbara, Jeffrey, Emily, Lynar and Jill for the kind of support and help that can't be expressed in words. Thank you all so much.

To our publisher, Peter Vegso at Health Communications, for believing in this journal, supporting this project and working hard to put it into the hands of millions of teenagers. Thank you, Peter.

To Lisa Drucker for her excellent editing skills and for being such a pleasure, in every sense of the word.

To Matthew Diener for his excellent editing skills, for answering endless questions and for being so good at what he does.

To Andrea Perrine Brower for her work on the cover, and to Dawn Grove for typesetting the manuscript.

To Craig Jarvie for his patience and for tolerating endless questions and requests.

A big thank-you to Terry Burke for his excellent sales work and his ability to keep us laughing.

To Lori Golden, Irene Xanthos and Jane Barone for believing in this project and for helping others believe in it.

To Kelly Maragni, Randee Goldsmith and Yvonne zum Tobel for their brilliant marketing.

To Kim Weiss, Ronni O'Brien and Larry Getlen for their wonderful and brilliant public relations efforts.

Thanks also to Karen Ornstein, Doreen Hess and Lisa Baxter for all they do at Health Communications to ensure that our customers are happy. A big thank-you to your staffs, as well.

Thanks to all the *Chicken Soup* coauthors who make it a joy to be a part of the *Chicken Soup* family: Patty Aubery, Marty Becker, Ron Camacho, Tim Clauss, Irene Dunlap, Patty Hansen, Jennifer Read Hawthorne, Carol Kline, Hanoch McCarty, Meladee McCarty, Nancy Mitchell, Maida Rogerson, Martin Rutte, Marci Shimoff, Barry Spilchuk and Diana von Welanetz Wentworth.

We are truly grateful for the many hands and hearts that made this journal possible. We love you all.

Introduction

Dear Teenager,

When *Chicken Soup for the Teenage Soul* was released in May of 1997 it was our deepest hope that you would love it and be inspired by it. We wanted you to know that you weren't alone on this journey and that all the feelings and doubts that you have are the same ones experienced by all teens. We wanted you to see that you were a normal teenager going through normal teen experiences. And, most important, we wanted you to know that you are loved. We feel we have succeeded.

Shortly after the book was released, we began receiving wonderful thank-you letters. Many of those letters included great stories or poems. We read each and every one of them. While doing so, we couldn't help but notice that after reading the book, you were inspired to write. You told us about lessons you learned and changes of heart you experienced after reading particular stories, and you wrote your own stories. You shared with us stories of your first love and your first break-up. You told us about your heartbreaks and heartaches with friends and family. You told us of your struggles with eating disorders and suicidal thoughts. You shared your grief about losing loved ones.

In short, *Chicken Soup for the Teenage Soul* inspired you to write about your life. This made us realize that the *Chicken Soup for the Teenage Soul Journal* was the next great thing we could offer you.

With this journal, you have the opportunity to create your own book. You can write your own stories and poems; you can answer questions and ask them. We have also included stories, poems and quotes—many of them written by other teenagers like you.

We have given you space to have your friends and family write to you about why they love you and which of your qualities they most admire. There are places for pictures of your boyfriend or girlfriend and of your friends. Last, but not least, we've given you lots of blank pages to fill in any way you like.

We have carefully chosen subject matters that concern you and questions that will enlighten you.

This journal is for you! Use it that way. Answer questions the way YOU want to, write about the things that interest you and skip over the things that don't. This isn't work, this is fun.

ENJOY!!

Share with Us

Allison (15) says, "What I liked best about the Journal was how the questions helped me to look at both sides of a situation. Usually I just see my side."

Ashley (14) says, "My favorite thing was that I could have my friends write things to me and then always have it to read if I wanted to."

We would love to know what you think about the *Chicken Soup for the Teenage Soul Journal.* Please share with us any ways that the *Journal* helped you or any ideas you have for making it better. Let us know what your favorite sections were and send us any entries you want to submit for future books. We are really excited to hear what you think and if you would like us to do a second volume of the *Journal.* We anxiously await your feedback and your stories.

We hope that you enjoy filling out this journal as much as we enjoyed putting it together. It was truly a labor of love.

Sharing & giving

Sharing — giving

Send letters and stories to:

Chicken Soup for the Teenage Soul
P. O. Box 936
Pacific Palisades, CA 90272
fax: 310-573-3657
e-mail: *letters@teenagechickensoup.com*
stories@teenagechickensoup.com
Web site: *www.teenagechickensoup.com*

I've finally stopped

running away

from myself.

Who else is there

better to be?

Goldie Hawn

Loving Yourself... Respect... Loving Yourself

*The hardest battle you're ever going to fight
is the battle to be just you.*

Leo Buscaglia

LOVING YOURSELF

It seems so much of my time and my energy have been focused on making or trying to make other people love me. The unspoken belief was that if I could make myself lovable to others I would feel loved.

Therefore, I spent much of my life trying to be more beautiful, skinnier, funnier, sweeter, and on and on. Every time I felt sad and not loved I would try to change something about myself, like, "I won't talk so much," or, "I will be less needy." Although both of these things would no doubt help, the point is, it isn't about what anyone else thinks of me. The truth is, I can only feel loved by others when I love myself. If I don't love myself, I will never feel loved.

Kimberly Kirberger

We are putting this chapter first because it is absolutely necessary to succeed at loving yourself before you can even begin to find happiness with others.

In this section, we will explore the way we talk to ourselves, the things we believe about ourselves and the things we can do to begin loving ourselves.

Loving yourself is different from being conceited or stuck-up. In fact, people who act conceited usually have a very low opinion of themselves.

Self-love is accepting yourself and treating yourself with gentle loving kindness. We seldom think about being understanding and forgiving "to ourselves," but it is **so** important.

Instead of beating up on yourself, try to treat yourself as you would your very dearest friend.

On the following pages you will explore what you like and don't like about yourself.

You will take a closer look at the way you talk to yourself and the way you treat yourself. Through close self-examination and lots of writing, you will begin the journey toward self-acceptance, and begin to develop and deepen the most important relationship of your life: your relationship with yourself.

To thine own self be true.

William Shakespeare

You must love yourself before you love another. By accepting yourself and fully being what you are, your simple presence can make others happy.
                                                    Jane Roberts

Make a list of all the things you like about yourself.

_____

_____

_____

_____

_____

_____

_____

_____

 _____

_____

_____

PICTURES OF ME

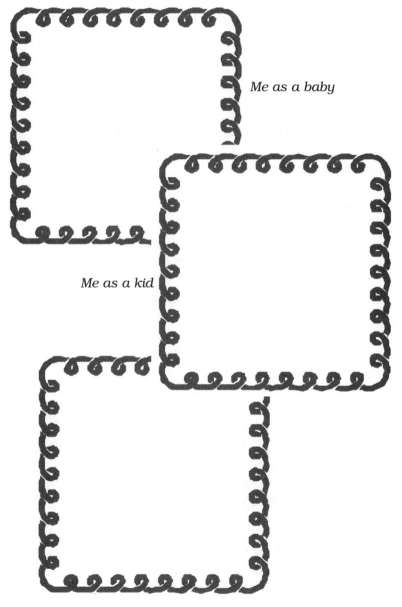

Me as a baby

Me as a kid

Me now

I Am . . .

I am a lemon with a twist,
I am a dewdrop full of mist,
I am a child filled with bliss,
I am but a gentle kiss,
I am invisible but I show,
I am a burned-out lamp that still does glow,
I am bold, though you may not know,
I am a horn that does not blow,
I am used, but still brand-new,
I am a mystery without a clue,
I am false, but forever true,
I am me and also you. . . .
I am a flower opening my buds,
I do not fight with fists, but with hugs,
I am a push without the shove,
Creeping, oh, so softly, I am love.
I am deaf, but I can hear,
I am afraid, but I have no fear,
I am forever constant throughout the year,
I am smart and my actions make it clear,
I am with the doll who was thrown in the corner,
I am at the funeral standing next to the mourner,
I am with the sad, small boy who people call a slow learner,
I stand beside the person who is rejected because he is a foreigner,
I hear the cry of a small boy saying his prayers,
I see the hearts of a million set up in flares,
I taste the bitter words and the nasty stares,
I can touch the small girl and feel her many tears,
I am with the stressed-out man living in strife,
I am in touch with the husband who lost his beloved wife,
I am stopping the man who is holding a knife,
Creeping, oh, so softly, I am life.

Khendi White

Make a list of all the things you don't like about yourself. (If you would feel more comfortable writing these on a separate piece of paper and then tossing it, that is fine. When you toss it, think to yourself, "I am getting rid of these negative thoughts about myself.")

_____

_____

_____

_____

_____

_____

_____

_____

_____

_____

_____

_____

_____

_____

_____

_____

What special talents do you have?

What are some of your favorite things to do?

Write a poem or story about yourself. Write it in the third person. Make it very positive and flattering. (Imagine your mom, your best friend and someone else who adores you are all writing it together.)

_____

_____

_____

_____

_____

_____

_____

_____

_____

_____

_____

_____

_____

_____

_____

*When someone comments on my weight,
I have to work hard to stand in front of the
mirror and say, "This is who you are.
You're okay in this body, and you're a great
healthy, lovable and loving person."
I try to accept myself.*

Rosie O'Donnell

Make a list of things you are self-conscious about.

_____

_____

_____

_____

_____

_____

_____

_____

_____

_____

TEENAGER

How to be?
How to stand?
What to wear?
Should I lend a hand?
When to laugh?
When to cry?
How to hide all that's inside?
To wear my hair low or high?
How to make the time rush by?
What to do?
When to speak?
How to stop my flushing cheeks?
How to say?
How to be?
Once and for all,
Who is me?

Jamie Newland

I would love and respect myself more if . . .

_____

_____

_____

_____

_____

_____

_____

_____

_____

Go through each thing you listed. If it is something you can change, make a promise to yourself to do so (e.g., "I gossip too much").

If it is something you can't change, make an effort to <u>accept</u> it.

Happiness cannot come from without.
It must come from within.

Helen Keller

MYSELF

I have to live with myself, and so
I want to be fit for myself to know,
I want to be able as days go by,
Always to look myself straight in the eye;
I don't want to stand, with the setting sun,
And hate myself for things I have done.

I don't want to keep on a closet shelf
A lot of secrets about myself,
And fool myself, as I come and go
Into thinking that nobody else will know
The kind of a person I really am;
I don't want to dress myself up in sham.

I want to go out with my head erect,
I want to deserve all people's respect;
But here in the struggle for fame and wealth
I want to be able to like myself.
I don't want to look at myself and know
That I'm bluster and bluff and empty show.

I can never hide myself from me;
I see what others may never see;
I know what others may never know,
I never can fool myself, and so,
Whatever happens, I want to be
Self-respecting and guilt-free.

Peer Counsellor Workbook

Forgiveness is a very powerful tool for increasing your love for yourself and your capacity to love others. To hold onto hateful feelings only poisons your own heart. Always try to forgive yourself and others.

Is there someone you need to forgive?

_____

_____

Is there someone you wish would forgive you?

_____

_____

Is there anything you need to forgive yourself for?

_____

_____

_____

_____

_____

If there are things about your past that are really bothering you, this could keep you from being able to be at peace with yourself.

Writing about these things helps. (Don't forget it also helps to talk to someone.)

Use these pages to clear up any past stuff that is bothering you.

_____

_____

_____

_____

_____

_____

_____

_____

_____

_____

_____

_____

_____

_____

_____

_____

_____

_____

*W*hatever you are doing, love yourself for doing it.
Whatever you are feeling, love yourself for feeling it.

Thaddeus Golas

It's important that we accept all of our feelings. What feelings do you have trouble accepting?

Do you accept your _____ sadness?

_____ anger?

_____ jealousy?

_____ envy?

_____ confusion?

_____ worry?

_____ excitement?

_____ anxiety?

_____ happiness?

_____ fear?

Reprinted by permission of Harley Schwadron.

Write about things that are difficult for you.

Example: "I have a hard time at parties when I don't know everyone," or "I am embarrassed by my mother's behavior."

_____

_____

_____

_____

_____

_____

_____

_____

_____

_____

_____

_____

_____

_____

*Love is not what we become,
but who we already are.*

Steven Levine

I believe that a human being in his natural state accepts everything about himself. This acceptance creates the most wonderful feeling of being in love with everything.

Kimberly Kirberger

On this page, explore the idea of total self-acceptance. You can write a story about it, a poem, or whatever you are inspired to do. Begin by imagining you are absolutely perfect, just the way you are. . . .

_____

_____

_____

_____

_____

_____

_____

_____

My Story . . . (continued)

My Story . . . (continued)

*To love oneself is the beginning
of a lifelong romance.*

Oscar Wilde

All About Me . . .

My favorite color_____

My favorite song_____

My favorite band _____

My favorite movie_____

My favorite TV show _____

My favorite teacher _____

My best talent_____

My best sport _____

My favorite subject_____

My favorite book_____

My favorite movie star _____

My favorite thing to do _____

My second-favorite thing to do _____

My favorite day of the week _____

All About Me . . . (continued)

My favorite Web site_____

Do you like your looks? _____

Do you like your body? _____

What is your best feature? _____

Describe yourself.

Length of hair_____

Color of hair _____

Color of eyes _____

Height _____

Are you athletic? _____

Are you healthy? _____

What emotion do you hide? _____

What is your favorite emotion?_____

Do you think you are smart? _____

What is your best subject? _____

What is your special talent? _____

What do you want to "be" when you "grow up"? _____

_____

Are you religious?_____

What is your religion? _____

All About Me . . . (continued)

Do you believe in God? _____

Do you get along well with people? _____

Are you fun? _____

Are you a good person?_____

What makes a person "a good person"? _____

_____

_____

_____

_____

_____

_____

_____

_____

_____

_____

_____

_____

_____

All About Me . . . (continued)

Name <u>one</u> thing you <u>would</u> change about yourself.

_____

_____

_____

Name <u>one</u> thing you <u>would not</u> change about yourself.

_____

_____

_____

For what are you grateful? _____

_____

_____

_____

_____

How would others describe you? _____

_____

_____

_____

_____

I AM

I am all I see.
Cobwebs shimmering in the trees,
Spiders crawling through the leaves,
Rivers, lakes, oceans and seas.
I am all I hear.
"Wash your face and clean your teeth,"
"She's your dog, you look after her,"
Rattlesnakes slithering through the sand,
Trombones and trumpets in a brass band.
I am all I feel.
Cool refreshing rain falling on my face,
The smooth soft feeling of cotton and lace,
The thump of my heart at its unsteady pace.
I am all I taste.
Soft warm bread that has just been baked,
The sweet sloppy mixture of chocolate cake.
I am all I remember.
My tenth birthday when I burnt my finger,
Memories of always wanting to be a singer.
I am all I've been taught.
Vowels A, E, I, O and U,
Grammar, spelling and safety rules.
I am all I think.
Fears I do not tell anyone of,
Like I'm an ugly duckling,
Who will one day be a swan.
I am the woman of the future.
I am all these things . . .
I accept all that life brings.

Kathryn Mockett

There are only two ways to live your life. One is as though nothing is a miracle. The other is as though everything is a miracle.

Albert Einstein

Gratitude is a very powerful feeling. It can heal great suffering.

Try this exercise: When you are feeling really bad and not loving yourself at all, begin to consciously change your thinking.

Think about the things you are grateful for (e.g., "My family cares for and loves me." "I am healthy." "I like that I am able to feel things deeply.").

Continue to think of all the things you are thankful for. After doing this for about ten minutes, stop and take a couple of deep breaths. See if you feel different.

Use the following page to list all the things you are grateful for. Keep coming back to it whenever you think of something new. After your list has grown, you can read it when you need to remind yourself of all your blessings.

_____

_____

_____

_____

_____

Gratitude

TO LOVE YOURSELF

It is wonderful to find someone you like or even love, but it is much more important to love yourself.

You may find great happiness in finding a friend who is a good and loyal person, but more happiness can be found in knowing that these things are true of you. It is great to meet people, who, just by being who they are, earn our love, appreciation, and respect; but it is greater to know that we deserve these things from the people in our lives.

Remember that the love, appreciation and respect that you feel for another are your feelings. They originate inside of you, and therefore, they belong to you. Remember that people come and go, and, of all the people in your life, you are the one who is there to stay. You are the one who can choose to love yourself, choose to respect yourself, and promise with all your heart and soul that you will never leave **you**.

Kimberly Kirberger

Once you are real,
you can't become unreal again.

Margery Williams
The Velveteen Rabbit

In order for us to become real, we need to learn to love ourselves. Once we do, we always will. Please be kind to yourself. Give yourself a break. Speak kindly and sweetly to yourself, the way you would speak to a beloved friend. You deserve it.

Use the following pages to explore loving and accepting yourself. Write about the daily discoveries you make about yourself. Write about things you do that make you feel good about yourself—choices that you make and help that you give. Once you start looking for the things about yourself that you like, you will find many. That is why we are giving you so many pages to use.

ENJOY THE JOURNEY.

Loving Yourself

_____

_____

_____

_____

_____

_____

_____

_____

_____

_____

_____

_____

_____

_____

_____

_____

_____

_____

_____

_____

Loving Yourself

_____

_____

_____

_____

_____

_____

_____

_____

_____

_____

_____

_____

_____

_____

_____

_____

_____

_____

_____

_____

Loving Yourself

_____

_____

_____

_____

_____

_____

_____

_____

_____

_____

_____

_____

_____

_____

_____

_____

_____

_____

_____

_____

_____

_____

_____

_____

_____

_____

_____

_____

_____

_____

_____

_____

_____

_____

_____

_____

_____

Loving Yourself

_____

_____

_____

_____

_____

_____

_____

_____

_____

_____

_____

_____

_____

_____

_____

_____

_____

_____

_____

Loving Yourself

_____

_____

_____

_____

_____

_____

_____

_____

_____

_____

_____

_____

_____

_____

_____

_____

_____

_____

Loving Yourself

_____

_____

_____

_____

_____

_____

_____

_____

_____

_____

_____

_____

_____

_____

_____

_____

_____

_____

_____

_____

_____

Loving Yourself

_____

_____

_____

_____

_____

_____

_____

_____

_____

_____

_____

_____

_____

_____

_____

_____

_____

_____

_____

Friendship

2.

...Friendship ... Friendship...

*A*nd in the sweetness of friendship

let there be laughter, and sharing

of pleasures.

Let your best be for your friend.

Kahlil Gibran

FRIENDSHIP

We think one of the greatest things about being a teenager is the sharing, the closeness and the great times that you have with your friends. Friends are a big and very important part of your life. They are the first ones you run to with good news and definitely the first ones you call with bad news. They are the ones you spend most of your time with and the ones with whom you share your hopes and dreams.

Friends, or the lack of them, are also a source of great pain and suffering. Nothing hurts worse than the betrayal or the loss of a friend.

We all have felt left out by a group of friends or not accepted by the "popular" group. And we all have been the ones to

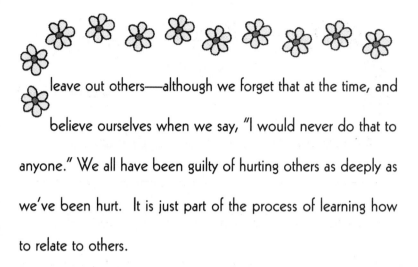

leave out others—although we forget that at the time, and believe ourselves when we say, "I would never do that to anyone." We all have been guilty of hurting others as deeply as we've been hurt. It is just part of the process of learning how to relate to others.

Use the following pages to write about what friendship means to you.

Write about your friends and what you like about them. Include the people you would like to have as friends but feel rejected by, and the people whom you reject. Write about the joys of friendship and the qualities you most enjoy in your friends. Use this chapter to explore and write about all aspects of yourself and your friendships.

A true friend is one who is there for you when he'd rather be anywhere else.

Len Wein

How would you describe a true friend?

_____

_____

_____

_____

_____

_____

_____

_____

_____

_____

_____

_____

_____

_____

Who is your best friend?

_____

_____

How did you meet?

_____

_____

_____

_____

Write about all the things you like about this person.

_____

_____

_____

_____

_____

_____

Pictures of my best friend

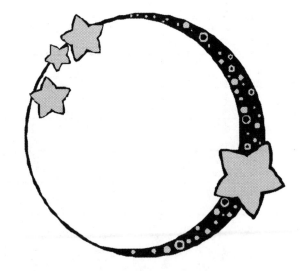

LET ME LEAN ON YOU

Keep your eyes upon me,
Keep me in your sight.
Help me down the crooked road,
Lead me to the light.
The road I'm on is dark
I'm not sure I know the way,
But with you beside me
I know I will not stray.
Protect me from the world I'm in
I'm certain we'll make it through,
Let me hold your hand
Let me lean on you.

Lissa Barker

Make a list of the qualities that you think make a person a good friend.

Pictures of my friends

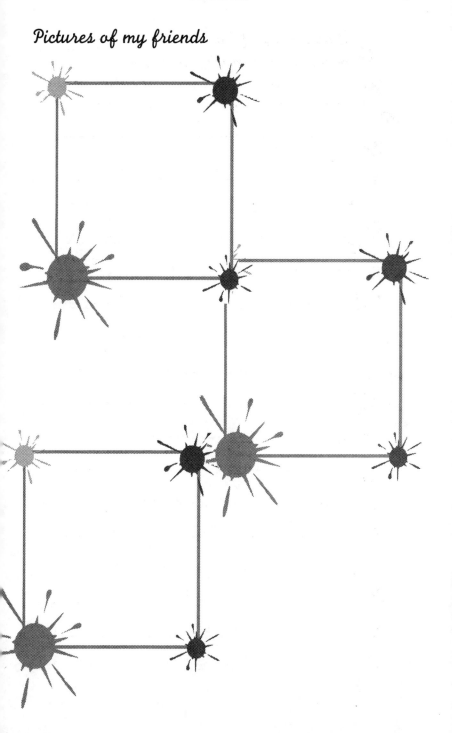

Are you a good friend? _____

Make a list of the things that make you a good friend.

_____

_____

_____

_____

_____

_____

_____

_____

_____

_____

What are the things you would like to improve about yourself as a friend?

_____

_____

_____

_____

_____

Thy friendship oft has made my heart to ache; do be my enemy— for friendship's sake.

William Blake

Make a list of things that mess up a friendship.

_____

_____

_____

_____

_____

_____

_____

_____

_____

_____

_____

_____

_____

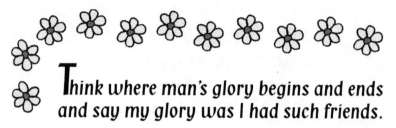

*Think where man's glory begins and ends
and say my glory was I had such friends.*

William Butler Yeats

Have your friends write to you on these pages
and tell you: What they like about you, what
makes you a good friend, a time you were really
"there" for them. Tell them you will turn to
these pages when you need some support and
when you need to remember they love you.

Friends Writing to Me . . . (continued)

_____

_____

_____

_____

_____

_____

_____

_____

_____

_____

_____

_____

_____

_____

_____

_____

_____

Friends Writing to Me . . . (continued)

Friends Writing to Me . . . (continued)

_____

_____

_____

_____

_____

_____

_____

_____

_____

_____

_____

_____

_____

_____

_____

_____

_____

_____

_____

Friends Writing to Me . . . (continued)

_____

_____

_____

_____

_____

_____

_____

_____

_____

_____

_____

_____

_____

_____

_____

_____

_____

_____

_____

_____

Friends Writing to Me . . . (continued)

_____

_____

_____

_____

_____

_____

_____

_____

_____

_____

_____

_____

_____

_____

_____

_____

_____

Friends Writing to Me . . . (continued)

Friends Writing to Me . . . (continued)

_____

_____

_____

_____

_____

_____

_____

_____

_____

_____

_____

_____

_____

_____

_____

_____

_____

Friends Writing to Me . . . (continued)

_____

_____

_____

_____

_____

_____

_____

_____

_____

_____

_____

_____

_____

_____

_____

_____

_____

_____

Friends Writing to Me . . . (continued)

_____

_____

_____

_____

_____

_____

_____

_____

_____

_____

_____

_____

_____

_____

_____

_____

Friends Writing to Me . . . (continued)

_____

_____

_____

_____

_____

_____

_____

_____

_____

_____

_____

_____

_____

_____

_____

_____

_____

Friendship is born at the moment when one person says to another "What! you too? I thought that no one but myself."

C. S. Lewis

Have you ever met anyone who was a lot like you?

_____

_____

_____

_____

_____

_____

_____

_____

_____

_____

_____

_____

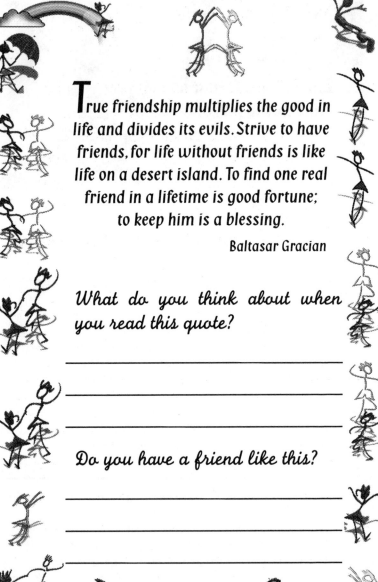

True friendship multiplies the good in life and divides its evils. Strive to have friends, for life without friends is like life on a desert island. To find one real friend in a lifetime is good fortune; to keep him is a blessing.

Baltasar Gracian

What do you think about when you read this quote?

_____

_____

_____

Do you have a friend like this?

_____

_____

_____

Sharing & giving

Sharing — giving

Each friend represents a world in us,
a world possibly not born until
they arrive, and it is only by
this meeting that a new world is born.

Anaïs Nin

When has a friend opened up a whole new world for you?

_____

_____

_____

_____

_____

_____

_____

_____

_____

_____

_____

_____

The most beautiful discovery true friends make is that they can grow separately without growing apart.

Elisabeth Foley

It is very difficult when a friend changes and goes in different directions than you. We have received thousands of letters from teenagers about this very issue. It is one of the most painful situations that growing up produces.

There are circumstances where growing apart does make it necessary for the friendship to end. However, there are many other types of growing where the friendship itself can grow and even become stronger.

Each situation is different, and the first step is to become clear on what the changes are and how they affect you.

Use these pages to write about friends who have changed and about the changes you have gone through. Then contemplate each situation and what the best possible solution may be.

Changes . . .

_____

_____

_____

_____

_____

_____

_____

_____

_____

_____

_____

_____

_____

_____

_____

_____

Changes . . . (continued)

_____

_____

_____

_____

_____

_____

_____

_____

_____

_____

_____

_____

_____

_____

_____

_____

N̲o distance of place or lapse of time can lessen the friendship of those who are thoroughly persuaded of each other's worth.

Robert Southey

I love this quote because it describes exactly how I feel about my best friend. We have had to go through some difficult changes and have been affected by our extremely busy schedules. For her, I will take the extra time, and will, indeed, do anything to maintain our friendship. I am convinced of her worth!

Kimberly Kirberger

Do you have a friend or friends whom you treasure so much that time and place cannot deter you from spending time together?

_____

_____

_____

Use this space to write about him or her or them.

_____

_____

_____

_____

_____

_____

Friends are people who help you
be more yourself.

Merle Shain

*Write about how your friends, or a friend,
help(s) you to be more yourself.*

_____

_____

_____

_____

_____

_____

_____

_____

_____

_____

_____

_____

_____

_____

You Tell On Yourself

You tell on yourself by the friends you seek,
By the very manner in which you speak,
By the way you employ your leisure time,
By the use you make of dollar and dime.

You tell what you are by the things you wear,
By the spirit in which your burdens you bear,
By the kind of things at which you laugh,
By the records you play on the phonograph.

You tell what you are by the way you walk,
By the things of which you delight to talk,
By the manner in which you bear defeat,
By so simple a thing as how you eat.

By the books you choose
from the well-filled shelf;
In these ways and more, you tell on yourself;
So there's really no particle of sense
In an effort to keep up a false pretense.

<u>Peer Counsellor Workbook</u>

Write a story about friendship.

Friendship Story . . . (continued)

_____

_____

_____

_____

_____

_____

_____

_____

_____

_____

_____

_____

_____

_____

_____

_____

_____

_____

_____

Make a list of all your friends and write one word next to each name that best describes that person.

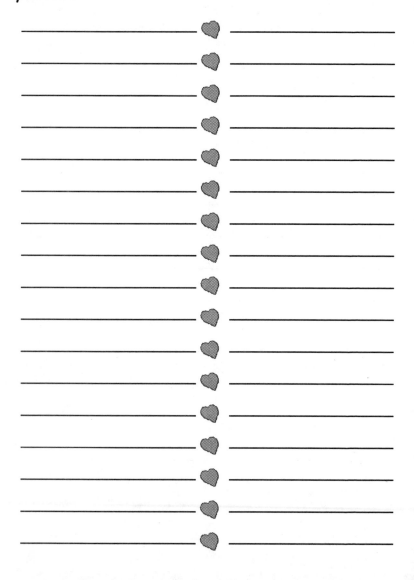

When have you felt left out by a group of friends?

_____

_____

_____

_____

_____

_____

How did it feel?

_____

_____

_____

_____

_____

What did you do about it?

_____

_____

_____

_____

Have you ever purposely excluded someone?

_____

_____

_____

_____

_____

How did it feel?

_____

_____

_____

_____

Did they do anything about it (e.g., say something to you or get mad)?

_____

_____

_____

_____

_____

_____

Have you ever found out that someone was talking meanly about you behind your back?

_____

_____

How did you feel?

_____

_____

_____

_____

_____

_____

_____

_____

Did you do anything about it (e.g., ask them about it)?

_____

_____

_____

_____

_____

Did you ever talk meanly about someone behind that person's back?

_____

_____

How did it feel?

_____

_____

_____

_____

_____

_____

Has it ever gotten you in trouble?

_____

_____

_____

If yes, how?

_____

_____

_____

Has a friend ever betrayed you?

_____

_____

_____

_____

_____

_____

Did you do anything about it (e.g., say something to them)?

_____

_____

_____

_____

_____

What?

_____

_____

_____

_____

_____

Have you ever betrayed a friend?

_____

_____

How?

_____

_____

How did it feel?

_____

_____

_____

_____

_____

Did your friend do anything about it (e.g., say something to you)?

_____

_____

_____

_____

Have any of your friends ever
had tragedies in their lives?

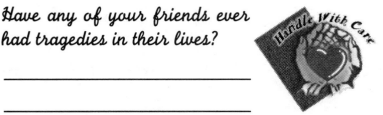

_____

_____

How did you help them?

_____

_____

_____

_____

How did it feel to help?

_____

_____

_____

_____

_____

_____

_____

_____

_____

Have you ever gone through something really difficult and had a friend help you through it?

Write about it.

_____

_____

_____

_____

_____

_____

_____

_____

_____

_____

_____

_____

_____

_____

_____

_____

_____

What have you learned about friendship from writing in your journal?

_____

_____

_____

_____

_____

_____

_____

What will you do differently?

_____

_____

_____

_____

_____

_____

_____

Sharing & giving

The following pages are blank for you to fill in however you wish.

Enjoy!

_____

_____

_____

_____

_____

_____

_____

_____

_____

_____

_____

_____

_____

_____

_____

_____

Friendship

Friendship

_____

_____

_____

_____

_____

_____

_____

_____

_____

_____

_____

_____

_____

_____

_____

_____

_____

_____

_____

_____

Friendship

Friendship

Friendship

Friendship

Friendship

Friendship

_____

_____

_____

_____

_____

_____

_____

_____

_____

_____

_____

_____

_____

_____

_____

_____

_____

_____

_____

_____

Relationships

3.

Relationships...Love...Caring...Tenderness

✳R·e·l·a·t·i·o·n·s·h·i·p·s

Love is patient and kind;
  love is not jealous, or
  conceited, or proud;
  love is not ill-mannered,
  or selfish, or irritable;
  love does not keep a
  record of wrongs; love is
  not happy with evil, but is
  happy with the truth.
  Love never gives up: its
  faith, hope and patience
  never fail.

1 Corinthians 13:4–7

RELATIONSHIPS

As a teenager, you are just beginning to experience this wonderful and challenging thing called "a relationship." In this chapter, we will explore your first crush, the first time you fell in love, and what it means to care about someone else in this way.

It is our experience that nothing is more wonderful or more difficult than a relationship. Nothing brings as much joy or as much pain. That is just the way it is.

Some of you may not have had a relationship yet, which is fine. We have no idea why some people always seem to be part of a couple and others find it close to impossible to "find someone," but it has little to do with how attractive you are.

In this section, you will explore liking and loving, dating and not dating, friends or more than friends, leaving and being left, growing apart, misunderstandings, different expectations and, of course, the best of all: dating bliss.

There is a section for your boyfriend or girlfriend to write to you, a place for pictures and room to write a story.

Hopefully, we have covered everything in this very important chapter, but just to be sure we have added lots of extra pages at the end of this section. Be creative, and remember, "love will find a way."

If you want to learn about love, start with plants and animals, they're easier.

Buddha

Do you have a boyfriend or girlfriend?

_____

_____

_____

_____

_____

_____

_____

Describe him or her.

_____

_____

_____

_____

_____

_____

_____

Do you not have a boyfriend or girlfriend, but wish that you did?

_____

_____

_____

_____

_____

_____

How do you feel about it?

_____

_____

_____

_____

_____

_____

Make a list of the qualities you want in a boyfriend or girlfriend.

For instance:
Caring
Romantic
Athletic

_____

_____

_____

_____

_____

_____

_____

_____

_____

_____

WARNING: This CD contains romantic lyrics which may cause you to fall in love with someone who is totally wrong for you and will make your life a nightmare.

Reprinted by permission of Randy Glasbergen.

Make a list of the qualities you bring to a relationship.

_____

_____

_____

_____

_____

_____

_____

_____

_____

_____

_____

_____

_____

_____

_____

_____

_____

_____

Use these pages to write about your boyfriend or girlfriend.

_____

_____

_____

_____

_____

_____

_____

_____

_____

_____

_____

Picture of my love

_____

_____

_____

_____

_____

_____

Life's greatest happiness is to be convinced
we are loved.

Victor Hugo

**Have your boyfriend or girlfriend use these pages
to write something to you.**

_____

_____

_____

_____

_____

_____

_____

_____

_____

_____

I Love You Because . . .

I Love You Because . . . (continued)

_____

_____

_____

_____

_____

_____

_____

_____

_____

_____

_____

_____

_____

_____

_____

_____

_____

In every living thing
there is the desire for love.

D. H. Lawrence

Have you ever had a crush on someone who only liked you as a friend?

_____

How did you feel?

_____

_____

_____

_____

What did you do?

_____

_____

_____

_____

_____

To love at all is to be vulnerable.

C. S. Lewis

Has there ever been someone who had a crush on you but you only liked him or her as a friend?

_____

How did you feel?

_____

_____

_____

_____

What did you do?

_____

_____

_____

_____

_____

_____

What is the nicest and most loving thing your boyfriend or girlfriend has ever done for you?

_____

_____

_____

_____

_____

_____

What is the nicest and most loving thing you have ever done for him or her?

_____

_____

_____

_____

_____

_____

_____

_____

What do you think is the meanest thing your boyfriend or girlfriend has ever done to you?

_____

_____

_____

_____

_____

What do you think is the meanest thing you have ever done to him or her?

_____

_____

_____

_____

_____

_____

_____

_____

_____

"FM-96 dedication line? The next time you test the Emergency Broadcast System, I'd like to dedicate it to my boyfriend because our relationship is a <u>disaster</u>!"

In your relationship:

What makes you jealous?

_____

_____

What makes you angry?

_____

_____

What hurts your feelings?

_____

_____

What makes you happy?

_____

_____

What makes you love him or her the most?

_____

_____

_____

_____

He who is in love is wise and is becoming wiser.

Ralph Waldo Emerson

What have you learned about love?

_____

_____

_____

_____

_____

_____

_____

_____

_____

_____

_____

_____

_____

Write about the first time you were in a relation-ship.

_____

_____

_____

_____

_____

_____

How did it end?

_____

_____

_____

_____

_____

_____

_____

_____

"I'm sorry we broke up and I was deeply hurt by the nasty poem you wrote me. On the other hand, I was very impressed that you were able to come up with thirty-seven words that rhyme with 'dork'!"

Have you ever thought you were never going to fall in love again?

_____

_____

_____

_____

_____

_____

What made you change your mind?

_____

_____

_____

_____

_____

_____

_____

"Hi, this is Cindy! To ask me out, press 1. To break up with me, press 2. To tell me I'm cute, press 3. . . ."

❤ ❤❤❤❤❤❤❤❤❤ ❤❤❤❤❤❤❤❤

Have you ever loved someone and pretended that you were just friends?

_____

_____

_____

_____

_____

_____

What were you afraid would happen if you told him or her the truth?

_____

_____

_____

_____

_____

❤ ❤❤❤❤❤❤❤❤❤ ❤❤❤❤❤❤❤❤

Do you ever wonder if a "friend" of yours is secretly in love with you?

_____

_____

_____

_____

_____

_____

What would you do if he or she told you that?

_____

_____

_____

_____

_____

_____

I hold it true, whate'er befall;
I feel it, when I sorrow most;
'Tis better to have loved and lost
Than never to have loved at all.

Alfred, Lord Tennyson

What is the best thing about being in a relationship?

_____

_____

_____

_____

_____

_____

_____

_____

_____

_____

What is the best thing about NOT being in a relationship?

_____

_____

_____

_____

_____

_____

_____

_____

_____

_____

_____

_____

_____

_____

Love does not consist in gazing at each other
but in looking outward together in the
same direction.

Antoine de Saint-Exupéry

Use the following pages to write all your feelings
about love and relationships.

_____

_____

_____

_____

_____

_____

_____

_____

_____

_____

. . . Loves me?

. . . Loves me not?

. . . Loves me?

. . . Loves me not?

. . . Loves me?

. . . Definitely loves me!

Relationships

_____

_____

_____

_____

_____

_____

_____

_____

_____

_____

_____

_____

_____

_____

_____

_____

_____

_____

Relationships

_____

_____

_____

_____

_____

_____

_____

_____

_____

_____

_____

_____

_____

_____

_____

_____

_____

_____

_____

Relationships

_____

_____

_____

_____

_____

_____

_____

_____

_____

_____

_____

_____

_____

_____

_____

_____

_____

Relationships

4.

Values—Growth

Gotta love 'em.

Jesse Kirberger, 12

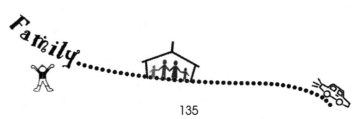

Family

135

FAMILY

When it comes to family, my twelve-year-old son, Jesse, says it best: "Gotta love 'em." He usually says that right after someone has done something silly and a bit annoying. He's right, too. There is something about family that makes us a little more forgiving.

When we are with our family, we are probably more our true selves than we are at any other time. Sometimes that means that we are more comfortable yelling and showing our anger or more apt to be total jerks, but the point is that no matter what we do, they just keep loving us and we them.

Kimberly Kirberger

As a teenager, some of your biggest challenges are with your parents. You are beginning to separate from them and become more independent. This is difficult for you and for them. You are also at an age when you begin to have different opinions, different priorities and different lifestyles.

Use these pages to write about these differences. Let yourself express your frustrations and contradictions. It is okay to have these feelings. It doesn't mean you don't love your parents; it is just part of growing up.

You may have parents who are divorced, or you may have lost a parent to death. These are difficult and challenging situations. Write about them. As you write, imagine that you are eliminating the pain and allowing your heart to begin healing.

Today's family comes in many different packages. Begin the work of accepting yours—and all its quirks—and your life will improve drastically.

There are also pages in this section for your parents, siblings and grandparents to write to you. You will treasure these pages forever, so take the time to ask each family member to write their feelings for you in this book.

I AM YOUR CHILD

I am your clay.

It is your firm but loving touch that will
shape me, my values and my goals.

I am your paper.

It is on me that your ideas and
feelings will be recorded, often
without your realizing it, and
carried on for many years.

I am your student.

It is through the help of your teachings and examples
that I will learn life's most important lessons.

I am your garden.

It is up to you to provide me with much-needed care
and attention, but, at the same time, room to grow.

I am your rainbow.

It is I who will bring you delight and joy after you've
been through a storm, if only you look closely.

I am your mirror.

It is in me that many parts of you will be reflected,
and if you've succeeded in doing your job, the image
will radiate beauty, warmth and love.

I am your child.

Denise Marigold

"I spoke with a social worker today.
If you keep playing '70s music, they're going
to put me in a foster home."

Reprinted by permission of Randy Glasbergen.

Describe your **FAMILY.**

_____

_____

_____

_____

_____

_____

_____

_____

_____

_____

_____

_____

_____

_____

_____

_____

_____

_____

_____

Make a list of the things you love and appreciate about your mother.

Make a list of the things that you and your mother disagree about.

Example: "I think I should be able to go out on school nights if I am home by 10 P.M. She thinks I should only go out on weekends."

_____

_____

_____

_____

_____

_____

Make a list of things you dislike about your mother.

_____   _____

_____   _____

_____   _____

_____   _____

_____   _____

_____   _____

_____   _____

Make a list of physical and character traits you inherited from your mother.

_____   _____

_____   _____

_____   _____

_____   _____

_____   _____

_____   _____

_____   _____

_____   _____

_____   _____

_____   _____

_____   _____

_____   _____

_____   _____

_____   _____

_____   _____

_____   _____

_____   _____

Use this space to write a poem and/or story about your mother.

_____

_____

_____

_____

_____

_____

_____

_____

_____

_____

_____

_____

_____

_____

_____

_____

Make a list of the things you love and appreciate about your father.

_____

_____

_____

_____

_____

_____

_____

_____

_____

_____

_____

_____

_____

_____

_____

_____

Make a list of the things you and your father disagree about.

_____

_____

_____

_____

_____

_____

_____

_____

Make a list of the things you dislike about your father.

_____   _____

_____   _____

_____   _____

_____   _____

_____   _____

Make a list of the physical and character traits you inherited from your father.

_____ _____

_____ _____

_____ _____

_____ _____

_____ _____

_____ _____

_____ _____

_____ _____

_____ _____

_____ _____

_____ _____

_____ _____

_____ _____

_____ _____

_____ _____

_____ _____

"I have low self-esteem because my mother was overly critical and my father never hugged me. That's why I drink from the toilet."

Use this page to write a poem and/or story about your father.

_____

_____

_____

_____

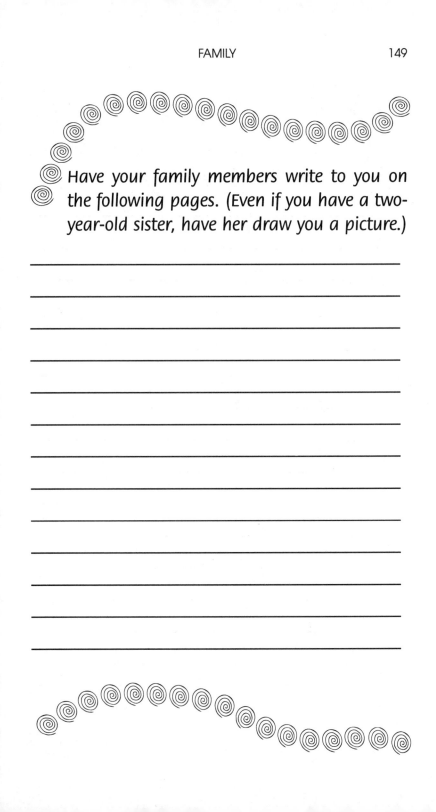

Have your family members write to you on the following pages. (Even if you have a two-year-old sister, have her draw you a picture.)

Family Writing to Me . . .

_____

_____

_____

_____

_____

_____

_____

_____

_____

_____

_____

_____

_____

_____

Family Writing to Me . . . (continued)

_____

_____

_____

_____

_____

_____

_____

_____

_____

_____

_____

_____

_____

_____

Family Writing to Me . . . (continued)

_____

_____

_____

_____

_____

_____

_____

_____

_____

_____

_____

_____

_____

_____

_____

_____

Family Writing to Me . . . (continued)

_____

_____

_____

_____

_____

_____

_____

_____

_____

_____

_____

_____

_____

_____

_____

_____

Family Writing to Me . . . (continued)

_____

_____

_____

_____

_____

_____

_____

_____

_____

_____

_____

_____

_____

_____

_____

_____

Family Writing to Me . . . (continued)

_____

_____

_____

_____

_____

_____

_____

_____

_____

_____

_____

_____

_____

_____

_____

PICTURES
OF
MY
FAMILY

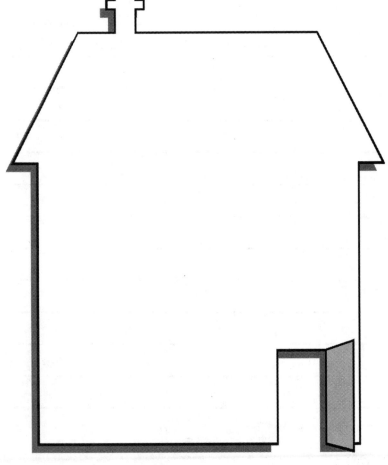

Do you have any siblings?

brothers_____

sisters_____

Are you the:

oldest ☐   youngest ☐   middle ☐

only child ☐

If you could change this, how would you have it be different?

_____

_____

_____

_____

Do you get along with your siblings?

_____

(Do you agree with us that "siblings" is a really strange word?!)

_____

What do you like best about your brother(s)?

_____

What do you like best about your sister(s)?

_____

_____

What do you like best about being an only child?

_____

_____

What do you dislike about your brother(s)?

_____

_____

What do you dislike about your sister(s)?

_____

_____

What do you dislike about being an only child?

_____

_____

Make a list of all the things you like, admire and respect about your family.

_____

_____

_____

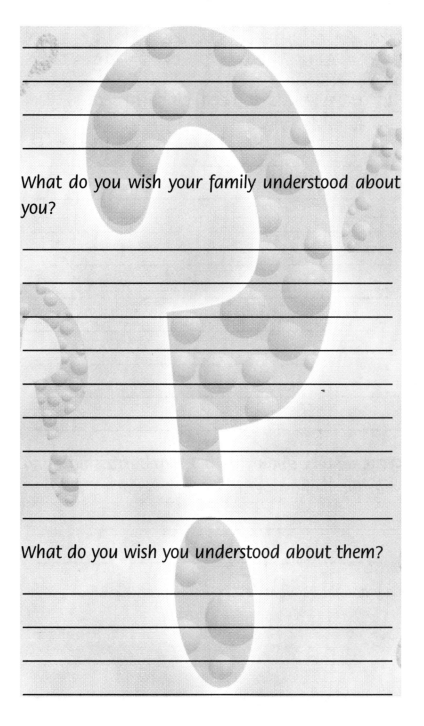

What do you wish your family understood about you?

What do you wish you understood about them?

Have you ever been embarrassed by your family?

_____

_____

_____

_____

_____

_____

_____

_____

Write a story about the most embarrassing thing your family has ever done.

_____

_____

_____

_____

 _____

_____

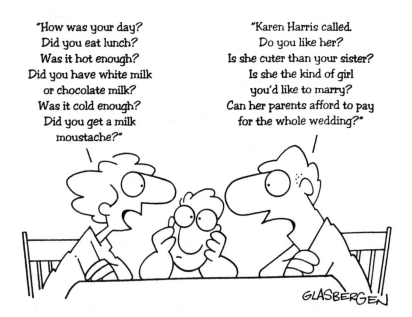

"You never pay any attention to me"—the words Jimmy will regret as long as he lives.

Reprinted by permission of Randy Glasbergen.

Kahlil Gibran says about children, "You may give them your love, but not your thoughts, for they have their own thoughts."

Do your parents try to make you think like they do?

_____

Give an example:

_____

_____

_____

_____

_____

  _____

Gibran goes on to say, ". . . seek not to make them like you."

Do you feel like your parents are trying to make you be like them?

_____

_____

_____

_____

Are you close to your grandparents?

_____

_____

Have you lost a grandparent?

_____

If you could tell your grandparents anything, what
would it be?

_____

_____

_____

_____

_____

_____

_____

_____

_____

_____

_____

_____

_____

Ask your grandparents to write something to you
on these pages. Let them know that you will
treasure their messages to you.

_____

_____

_____

_____

_____

_____

_____

_____

_____

_____

_____

_____

_____

_____

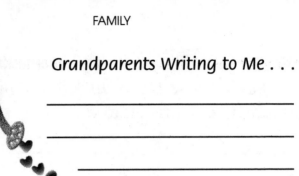

Grandparents Writing to Me . . .

_____

_____

_____

_____

_____

_____

_____

_____

_____

_____

_____

_____

_____

_____

_____

_____

_____

_____

_____

_____

_____

Grandparents Writing to Me . . . (continued)

_____

_____

_____

_____

_____

_____

_____

_____

_____

_____

_____

_____

_____

_____

_____

_____

_____

_____

_____

_____

The following is the journal entry of a young girl.

She has told us that writing has been her salvation, that many times when she thought no one could understand what she was going through, paper was her best friend. We chose her example because she is able to express her feelings. Paper is such a safe place to do that. If we can allow ourselves to feel our feelings, we can begin to <u>feel better</u>. Let these pages be a friend that you can turn to with whatever feelings you have.

HURRICANE DIVORCE

October 30, 1989

Dear Diary,

My parents are getting a divorce. . . . My father is a big idiot. He's mean, obnoxious and horrible. I hate him. All he does is scribble in his retarded journal, stuff to show his lawyer. He slams doors and yells at Mommy. I wish he'd shut up and get lost.

This is the diary entry of an angry, confused and frustrated ten-year-old girl: me.

Imagine for a moment what it might feel like to be in the middle of a hurricane. The winds howling all around you, cold raindrops sliding down your face, everything falling apart from the powerful strength the storm possesses. Half of all marriages end in divorce and anyone who has lived through one knows this helpless, hopeless feeling.

It was six years ago that I scrawled those words in my childish penmanship but even today, the first word that comes to my mind when I think of my parents' divorce is nightmare. Indeed it was a nightmare, filled with screaming, crying, brainwashing, desertion and never-ending pain . . . only I couldn't wake up because it was real.

I remember constantly changing my mind over which parent's side to take. It was either "I love Mommy, I hate Sam" or "I love Daddy, I hate Lynn." Calling my parents by their first names was my method of separation and disassociation.

It was a time of hypocrisies, lies and contradictions. I remember my father telling me horrible things about my mother. And my mother telling me over and over again that Sam was a sick, twisted monster who didn't love me. . . . Never had, never would.

One day in fifth grade, I hadn't done my homework. My teacher was annoyed, but little did she know I had spent the night with my mother in a hotel because the order of protection against my father had yet to come through. I felt as if I were drowning in an ocean of tears.

I could go on forever describing that time in my life, but these days I'm trying to move past all that. The winds of hatred have begun to calm around me, and sometimes I can see the sun peeking out from behind the rain clouds of my painful memories.

Carrie Cohen

Use the following pages to write about any difficulties you are having with your family. You may want to vent your anger or explore your deep feelings of rebellion. You may also want to write about more positive feelings. We received a letter from a girl who wrote: "I'm always fighting with my mom, but I love her so much. I wish I could get along with her. I'm going to try to not get mad so easily." Remember emotions are as ever-changing as the weather, but it helps to write them down as a means of moving past them.

Family

Family

Family

Family

_____

_____

_____

_____

_____

_____

_____

_____

_____

_____

_____

_____

_____

_____

_____

_____

_____

_____

_____

_____

Family

Family

_____

_____

_____

_____

_____

_____

_____

_____

_____

_____

_____

_____

_____

_____

_____

_____

_____

_____

_____

_____

_____

_____

Family

Family

Family

5.

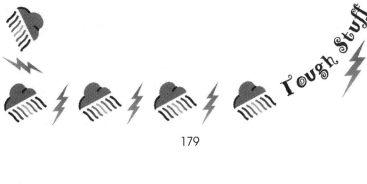

There is a great deal of pain in life and perhaps the only pain that can be avoided is the pain that comes from trying to avoid pain.

R. D. Laing

TOUGH STUFF

As I write this, only ten days have passed since one of my dearest friends took his life. Anger, hurt, devastation, regret, sorrow, searing pain . . . only begin to describe my feelings. I am aware of how I try to find thoughts, theories and beliefs that will explain it, that will make it easier—and, yet, there aren't any. Death is a profound teacher, though, and I have learned a lot from this. I have learned that whenever the question is "What is important?"; the answer is always "Love."

Other loved ones in my life have died. My husband when he was thirty-eight and my best friend when she was thirty. Each time I found myself feeling the same thing: All that mattered was the love we had for one another. Each time I hurt because I could no longer give my love to that person and I could no longer receive that person's love for me. Or so it seemed to me at the time.

The truth is, we can help each other even after death. I can love my friend's children and I can protect my husband's memory through our child. Every day I am given opportunities to give love to those who have passed away.

Life is filled with tough stuff. Death, illness and other causes of human suffering are all part of life. Although extremely difficult, these are the situations that produce the deepest and most profound growth. For some reason, we are more open to learning when we are hurting. We are softer—we are able to admit that we don't know everything. Especially during these times, it is *so* important to remember to love ourselves.

Kimberly Kirberger

When faced with painful realities, it always helps to talk about them. Don't let yourself believe, "No one wants to hear about my problems" or "It is too uncomfortable to talk about something so awful." The more fear you have of discussing it, the more important it is to do so. Please, we beg of you: talk, talk, talk.

It can also be very comforting to write about "tough stuff." Write about every aspect of your suffering, your challenges and your trials. Write about all the feelings, write about the hard lessons you've learned and write about your hopes and prayers for the future.

Please know that you are not alone. There are many people who care.

At the back of the book there are phone numbers of hotlines, plus some suggested reading.

Please refer to our Web site, *www.teenage chickensoup.com* for ongoing support with tough stuff. There you will find opportunities to discuss difficult issues with other teens, as well as monthly live chats with therapists and with coauthor Kimberly Kirberger. Contact Kimberly Kirberger's office at 310-573-3655 for more information about this Web site.

If you think you might need to talk to someone . . . please do! WE LOVE YOU!!

Although the world is full of suffering, it is also full of overcoming it.

Helen Keller

Make a list of the most difficult things you have experienced.

_____

_____

_____

_____

_____

_____

_____

_____

_____

_____

_____

_____

Have you ever had anyone close to you die?

_____

How did you find out?

_____

_____

Did you get to say good-bye?

_____

Did you go to the funeral?

_____

What was it like?

_____

_____

Have you ever known anyone your age who died?

_____

How did it feel?

_____

_____

Did it scare you?

_____

TERRIFIED TEARS

The face of an angel is all that is here,
One beautiful freckle equals one terrified tear.
Not ready to leave but has to go,
Wants to go back but God says no.
Leaving your life is a scary thought,
I guess it's something that can't be fought.
A mother, a father, a sister, and friends,
A meaningful life that suddenly ends.
An angel is what she was meant to be,
Now just think of all she can see.
Looking over her family night and day,
Saying I love you in her own special way.
In the night we sleep, in the day we cry.
She watches us all from her star in the sky.

Lyndsie Chlowitz
Dedicated with love to Sabrina

If you could send a message to someone who has passed on, what would it be? Use this space to write your message.

_____

_____

_____

_____

_____

_____

_____

_____

_____

_____

_____

_____

_____

_____

_____

_____

_____

LIFE

The snow will fall, the ground gets cold,
A baby's born who will grow old.
A blanket of snow covers the ground,
Still the answer is not found.

A bird will chirp, the grass grows green,
And through the clouds the sun is seen.
The flowers bloom, the bees will buzz,
The world again as it once was.

The sun will shine, the day is long,
The birds they sing an endless song.
The sky is bright, the color blue,
A child knows who never knew.

A breeze is felt and with a chill,
The song has stopped that never will.
The leaves will fall, the color red,
A whistle of the wind is all that's said.

Why it happens all this way,
That is not for me to say.
A baby's born who someday dies,
But from the clouds the sun will rise.

Danielle Rosenblatt

THE "TOUGH STUFF" QUESTIONNAIRE

Have you ever been really sick?

_____

_____

Is anyone in your family really sick?

_____

_____

Has anyone close to you died?

_____

_____

Have you ever been in the hospital?

_____

_____

Have your parents or siblings ever been hospitalized?

_____

_____

Do you have an eating disorder?

_____

_____

THE "TOUGH STUFF" QUESTIONNAIRE (continued)

Have you ever had an eating disorder?

_____

_____

Do you have a drug problem?

_____

_____

Do you have a drinking problem?

_____

_____

Does anyone in your family have a drug problem?

_____

_____

Does anyone in your family have a drinking problem?

_____

_____

Are your parents divorced?

_____

_____

Do your parents fight constantly?

_____

_____

THE "TOUGH STUFF" QUESTIONNAIRE (continued)

Do your parents talk about getting divorced?

_____

_____

Have you ever run away from home?

_____

_____

Have you ever been physically abused?

_____

_____

Have you ever been sexually abused?

_____

_____

Have you ever attempted suicide?

_____

_____

Have you ever thought about suicide?

_____

_____

Do you have any friends who have committed suicide?

_____

_____

_____

THE "TOUGH STUFF" QUESTIONNAIRE (continued)

Do you have any friends who have attempted to commit suicide?

_____

_____

Have you ever driven a car while drunk?

_____

_____

Have you ever been in a car that was being driven by someone who was drunk?

_____

_____

Do you know anyone who has died in a car accident caused by a drunk driver?

_____

_____

Have you ever witnessed extreme suffering?

_____

_____

Have you ever experienced extreme suffering?

_____

_____

_____

THE "TOUGH STUFF" QUESTIONNAIRE (continued)

How do you feel when you see a homeless person?

_____

_____

Do you ever wonder why there is so much suffering?

_____

_____

Do you believe that pain makes us grow?

_____

_____

_____

_____

_____

_____

_____

_____

_____

_____

_____

_____

_____

_____

_____

_____

Well ... if you got through that, you probably could use some cheering up. Put on your favorite music and dance around your room and sing really loud. (Who cares? Sometimes you just have to be crazy.) Use the pages at the end of this chapter to write about anything that has been difficult for <u>you</u>! As you write, imagine that anything you put down on paper will instantly be less painful. Whenever we take the darkness from inside ourselves and expose it to the light, we "lighten up." Try it!

*T*hat which hurts, also
        instructs.

Ben Franklin

What have you learned from your pain?
Make a list of difficult situations and
write next to them what you learned.

_____

_____

_____

_____

_____

_____

_____

_____

_____

_____

_____

_____

_____

_____

Learning from Pain ...

Your pain is the breaking of the shell that encloses your understanding.

Kahlil Gibran

What kinds of things cause you pain?

_____

_____

_____

Do you let yourself feel your emotional pain or do you try to make it go away?

_____

_____

Next time you are in pain try to just relax into it and feel it. Then write in here about what that was like. . . .

_____

_____

_____

_____

_____

_____

*M*uch of your pain is self-chosen.
It is the bitter potion by which the physician
within you, heals your sick self.

Kahlil Gibran

What does this quote mean to you?

_____

_____

_____

Are there things you do that you later feel you did so you could learn a lesson?

_____

_____

Describe one.

_____

_____

_____

What did you learn?

_____

_____

What is the biggest mistake you have ever made?

_____

_____

When did you do something even though you knew it would cause you pain?

_____

_____

When did you not do something because you knew it would cause you pain?

_____

_____

Did you ever do something that you knew would cause someone else a great deal of pain?

_____

_____

Did you ever choose not to do something because you knew it would hurt someone else?

_____

_____

_____

To every thing there is a season,
and a time to every purpose
under heaven.
A time to be born, and a time to die;
a time to plant, and a time to
pluck up that which is planted;
A time to kill, and a time to heal;
a time to break down,
and a time to build up;
A time to weep, and a time to laugh;
a time to mourn, and a time to dance;
A time to cast away stones,
and a time to gather stones together;
A time to embrace,
and a time to refrain from embracing;
A time to get, and a time to lose;
a time to keep, and a time to cast away;
A time to rend, and a time to sew;
a time to keep silence,
and a time to speak;
A time to love, and a time to hate;
a time of war,
and a time of peace.

Eccles. 3:1-8

What doesn't kill me, makes me stronger.

Nietzsche

Describe a painful situation that made you stronger.

_____

_____

_____

_____

_____

_____

_____

_____

_____

_____

_____

_____

_____

_____

*We are healed of a suffering
only by experiencing
it to the full.*

Marcel Proust

Write a story about experiencing a very
difficult situation "to the full" and being
healed by "fully feeling it."

_____

_____

_____

_____

_____

_____

_____

_____

_____

_____

_____

_____

_____

_____

Choose Life

Life is precious,
But God takes it away—
Why, we just don't know.
And in time we come to accept
That it was their time to go.
But what happens
When one takes his or her own life,
Leaving loved ones in despair—
Why did this person not understand:
There are people here who care.
Peers understand it's hard to cope
When pressures get too great,
But choosing death should not be
Your only choice or fate.
So when life's problems get you down
And you cannot see the end,
Find the time to call someone—
A buddy, peer, or friend.

Lilian Gamble

Have you ever thought about suicide?

_____

_____

Describe how you felt.

_____

_____

What did you do?

_____

_____

_____

_____

_____

_____

_____

We urge you to make a promise to yourself that you won't ever think of this as a solution!! There is a saying, "Suicide is a permanent solution to a TEMPORARY problem." Seek instead a temporary solution: call someone, cry, yell, eat too much ice cream. Make a pact with a friend or an adult that if you ever feel suicidal, you will call them or visit with them IMMEDIATELY.

Write here what advice you would give to someone who is feeling suicidal.

_____

_____

_____

_____

_____

_____

_____

_____

_____

_____

_____

_____

_____

_____

_____

_____

_____

Tough Stuff

Advice ...(continued)

_____

_____

_____

_____

_____

_____

_____

_____

_____

_____

_____

_____

_____

_____

_____

_____

_____

_____

_____

Tough Stuff

_____

_____

_____

*Instead of weeping when a tragedy occurs
in a songbird's life, it sings away its grief.
I believe we could well follow the pattern
of our feathered friends.*

                                        Robert S. Walker

*Use the following pages to "sing away your grief." Write
about all the things that cause you pain and all the difficult
experiences you have had to live through in your life. Think
of the healing that is happening as you bring the pain out
of its dark hiding places into the light. Once again remember:
you are not alone.*

_____

_____

_____

_____

_____

_____

_____

_____

_____

_____

Tough Stuff

Tough Stuff

_____

_____

_____

_____

_____

_____

_____

_____

_____

_____

_____

_____

_____

_____

_____

_____

_____

_____

_____

_____

Tough Stuff

_____

_____

_____

_____

_____

_____

_____

_____

_____

_____

_____

_____

_____

_____

_____

_____

_____

_____

_____

_____

Tough Stuff

_____

_____

_____

_____

_____

_____

_____

_____

_____

_____

_____

_____

_____

_____

_____

_____

_____

_____

_____

_____

_____

_____

Tough Stuff

Tough Stuff

Tough Stuff

_____

_____

_____

_____

_____

_____

_____

_____

_____

_____

_____

_____

_____

_____

_____

_____

_____

_____

_____

_____

_____

_____

_____

Love and Kindness

6.

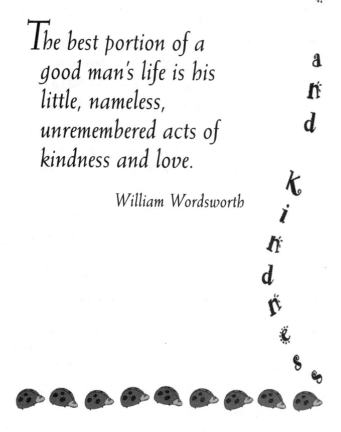

Love and Kindness
Love and Kindness

*T*he best portion of a
good man's life is his
little, nameless,
unremembered acts of
kindness and love.

William Wordsworth

LOVE AND KINDNESS

Love and Kindness: the true key to happiness. It is interesting how we often think that our happiness will come from others doing something kind for us or others loving us, but the truth is more happiness comes from our doing something kind for another and our feeling love for another. There is a quote that says, "love isn't love until you give it away." It's as if in order to feel the good feelings that come with love, you have to give them to another.

So many of the <u>Chicken Soup</u> stories are about love and kindness. The huge success of these books is due to the fact that people feel good when they read about other people being loving and kind. When a person is being kind, he is operating at his highest potential. The same is true when a person is feeling love, whether it be for another or for life in general.

As a teenager, these feelings are very strong for you. Friendships and relationships are a huge part of your life and with them come many opportunities to show love and kindness. At the same time, these feelings can be awkward to express. It isn't always easy to say "I care, let me help you." We all worry, "What if the other person laughs at me or doesn't want my help?" At times, we all can feel uncomfortable receiving love and kindness, too. Let's face it, sometimes it is easier just to be the tough guy who doesn't get into all that sentimental stuff.

It is worth the risk, though, because allowing ourselves to be vulnerable and to feel love and kindness for and from others is the very thing we are all looking for. It really is THE KEY TO HAPPINESS.

*L*ord, make me an instrument of
Your peace.
Where there is hatred
let me sow love;
where there is injury, pardon;
where there is doubt, faith;
where there is despair, hope;
where there is darkness, light;
and where there is sadness,
Oh, Lord, give me joy.

Saint Francis of Assisi

*E*very human feels pleasure in doing good to another.

Thomas Jefferson

Do you agree with this quote?

_____

Why do you think this is true?

_____

_____

What are some examples of acts of kindness?

_____

_____

_____

_____

Make a list of some acts of kindness you have done recently.

No act of kindness,
however small, is ever wasted.

IDEA:

Every day, perform an act of kindness without letting
the recipient know it was you. Make a list of some
different possibilities here, and when you do them,
check them off.

(Pay attention to how difficult it is not to tell the person
that it was you.)

_____

_____

_____

_____

_____

_____

_____

_____

_____

_____

_____

*Each one of us has the power
to make others feel better or worse.
Making others feel better is much more fun
than making others feel worse.
Making others feel better
generally makes us feel better.*

Laura Huxley

_____

_____

_____

_____

_____

_____

_____

_____

_____

The heart has eyes which the brain knows nothing of.

Charles Perkhurst

So often, we spend the day seeing the world from our minds. We judge, worry, analyze—and on and on. Every now and then, we have days that are somehow different—better. We feel compassion for others and assume the best instead of the other way around. Those are the days when we are thinking with our hearts more than with our minds.

Try spending a day "seeing with your heart" instead of your mind. This is a big challenge and you will forget more than you will remember, but that is okay. Try to be compassionate rather than judgmental. Try to be kind to the person you normally ignore. Try to appreciate your teachers' hard work and take a minute to speak to your parents.

As you do this exercise, be aware of how the world treats you back.

At the end of the day, write about it. Write about how you felt and if people seemed to treat you better. Write about the smiles you brought to people and to yourself.

My Day of Seeing with My Heart ...

_____

_____

_____

_____

_____

_____

_____

_____

_____

_____

_____

_____

_____

_____

_____

The greatest gift is a portion of thyself.

Ralph Waldo Emerson

We read a story recently by a girl who was trying to decide what to give her mom for Christmas. After looking everywhere and finding nothing that really impressed her, she realized what it was her mom really wanted from her. She wanted to spend time with her. Instead of a present, the girl gave her mom a coupon worth "a day together," doing whatever her mom wanted.

So often this is the case. People want a portion of us, but instead, we think we need to buy something for them.

Use this page to write about people in your life who most likely want to spend time with you. If you end up calling them and spending time together, write about it here.

PLEASE LOOK A LITTLE DEEPER

Please don't judge me by my face,
By my religion or my race.
Please don't laugh at what I wear,
Or how I look or do my hair.
Please look a little deeper—
Way down deep inside,
And although you may not see it,
I have a lot to hide.
Behind my clothes, the secrets lie,
Behind my smile, I softly cry.
Please look a little deeper,
And maybe you will see
The lonely little girl
That lives inside of me.
Please listen carefully to her—
She'll show that she's insecure.
Please try to be a friend to her
And show her that you care.
Please just get to know her
And maybe you will see
That if you just look deep enough,
You'll find the real me.

Tiffany Trutenko

Write about a time when you helped someone.

_____

_____

_____

_____

_____

_____

_____

_____

_____

_____

_____

_____

_____

_____

_____

_____

Write about a time when someone helped you.

_____

_____

_____

_____

_____

_____

_____

_____

_____

_____

_____

_____

_____

_____

_____

READER/CUSTOMER CARE SURVEY

If you are enjoying this book, please help us serve you better and meet your changing needs by taking a few minutes to complete this survey. Please fold it and drop it in the mail.

PLEASE PRINT C8K

NAME:

ADDRESS:

TELEPHONE NUMBER:

FAX NUMBER:

E-MAIL:

(1) Gender: 1) ____ Girl 2) ____ Boy

(2) Age:
1) ____ 8 or under
2) ____ 9-12
3) ____ 13-16
4) ____ 17-20
5) ____ 21-30
6) ____ 31-40
7) ____ 41-50
8) ____ 51+

(3) Who purchased this book?
1) ____ You
2) ____ Parent
3) ____ Grandparent
4) ____ Friend
5) ____ Relative
6) ____ Adult Friend
7) ____ Counselor or Teacher

(4) Was this book bought as a gift?
1) ____ Yes
2) ____ No

(5) How did you find out about this book?
1) ____ Friend
2) ____ School
3) ____ Parent
4) ____ Radio
5) ____ Counselor
6) ____ Teen magazine Ad
7) ____ Newspaper or magazine review

(8) What do you like to read?

Teen magazines:
8) ____ Teen
9) ____ Seventeen
10) ____ Teen People
11) ____ YM
12) ____ Jump
13) ____ Teen Beat
14) ____ All About You
15) ____ Twist
16) ____ Christian Youth Magazines
17) ____ Comics

Books:
18) ____ Young Adult Fiction
19) ____ Romance
20) ____ Self-help
21) ____ Sci-fi

(22) Where do you usually buy books?
1) ____ Bookstore
2) ____ Discount Store
3) ____ Grocery Store
4) ____ School Book Sale
5) ____ Web Sites
6) ____ Price Club

(23) How many Chicken Soup books have you bought or read?
1) ____ 1
2) ____ 2
3) ____ 3
4) ____ 4+

As a special **"Thank You"** we'll send you news about new books and a valuable Gift Certificate!

(24) What are your TWO favorite TV Shows?
1) ____ Dawson's Creek
2) ____ Beverly Hills 90210
3) ____ Boy Meets World
4) ____ 7th Heaven
5) ____ The Simpsons
6) ____ Sabrina the Teenage Witch
7) ____ Buffy the Vampire Slayer
8) ____ Party of Five
9) ____ Other

Describe a book that you would like to buy especially for teens that isn't currently available

BUSINESS REPLY MAIL
FIRST-CLASS MAIL PERMIT NO 45 DEERFIELD BEACH, FL

POSTAGE WILL BE PAID BY ADDRESSEE

CHICKEN SOUP FOR THE TEEN/KID'S SOUL
HEALTH COMMUNICATIONS, INC.
3201 SW 15TH STREET
DEERFIELD BEACH FL 33442-9875

FOLD HERE

Thank You!!

Do you have your own Chicken Soup story you would like to send us?
Please send it separately to:
Chicken Soup for the Soul,
P.O. Box 30880, Santa Barbara, CA 93130

Additional Comments:

_____
_____
_____
_____
_____
_____

C8K

The following pages are blank. Use them to write about love and kindness and any thoughts, stories or poems that go with them.

Also, you can ask a friend to write something on these pages, perhaps about a time when he or she received love and kindness from you, or vice versa.

Be creative. Explore and fill these pages—and your life—with love and kindness.

_____

_____

_____

_____

_____

_____

_____

_____

_____

_____

_____

_____

_____

_____

_____

_____

Learning Lessons

7.

LEARNING LESSONS

An <u>is</u> *is just a* <u>was</u> *that was*
and that is very small ...
And <u>is</u> *is* <u>was</u> *so soon*
it almost wasn't <u>is</u> *at all*
For is is only <u>is</u> *until*
<u>it</u> *is a* <u>was</u>*—you see....*
And as an <u>is</u> *advances—to*
remain an <u>is</u> *can't be*
'cause if is is to stay an <u>is</u>
it isn't <u>is</u> *because*
another <u>is</u> *is where it was*
and <u>is</u> *is then a* <u>was</u>*.*

Tom Hicks

Life lessons . . . EDUCATION . . . LOVING YOURSELF . . . Life Lessons . . . .

235

LEARNING LESSONS

The reason we picked this poem to go with learning lessons is because of how important it is to realize that an IS soon becomes a WAS. One of the ways we learn in life is through our mistakes.

Say, for instance, you were mean to a friend. You feel terrible and think, *I am a mean person.* This is not going to help you as much as thinking, ***I am a nice person who WAS mean to a friend. I will apologize and I will remember that I feel badly when I am mean to my friends.***

Learning lessons is often a painful experience, but it doesn't have to be. We can learn a lot from our mistakes, but we can also learn from the things we do right. One way to ensure that this happens more often is to let yourself feel good when you do something right (e.g., "I finished all my homework before dinner. Now I will be able to relax and I won't dread going to school tomorrow.") Let yourself really experience how good that feels, and you will learn that doing what you need to do feels good.

In the cases where you learn from mistakes or painful situations, just be sure not to beat yourself up too much. Try to learn the lesson and move on. Let an IS become a WAS.

Use this chapter to write down lessons you would rather not have to learn over and over. Also use it to discover what lesson is hidden in a given situation.

There will be plenty of room at the end of the chapter for exploring these things further.

Remember: "An IS is just an is that WAS and that is very small!"

*Tell me, I'll forget. Show me, I may remember.
But involve me and I'll understand.*

Chinese Proverb

Do you think people learn from their mistakes?

_____

Do you think people can learn "the easy way"?

_____

Have you ever learned anything the easy way?

_____

What?

_____

Have you ever had to learn something the hard way?

_____

What?

_____

Is there a lesson that you know you haven't quite learned yet?

_____

What is it?

_____

_____

There is no way to know before experiencing.

Dr. Robert Anthony

What is the most difficult thing you have gone through in your life?

_____

_____

What did you learn from it?

_____

_____

_____

_____

_____

_____

_____

_____

_____

_____

_____

_____

_____

Have you learned lessons from happy situations?

_____

_____

Give some examples.

_____

_____

_____

_____

_____

_____

Do you try to learn from painful situations?

_____

_____

Give some examples.

_____

_____

_____

_____

_____

_____

Do you believe things happen for a reason?

_____

_____

_____

_____

_____

_____

_____

_____

What is the most important lesson you have ever learned?

_____

_____

_____

_____

_____

_____

_____

_____

_____

OUT OF THE POTHOLES

While shuffling down the road one day, a turtle fell into a large pothole in the center of a country road. Spinning his little legs to free himself proved futile, to say the least. Soon a rabbit friend came hopping by and offered his assistance. But no matter what they tried, the turtle remained stuck in the muddy hole. "It's no use," the turtle said. "Nothing will ever free me." Other friends passed his way, but the turtle refused their help, for he believed his destiny included death in the muddy mire. Therefore, he withdrew his head inside the safety of his shell. "It's hopeless," he lamented, but suddenly he heard a loud noise. Peeking from his internal home, the turtle spotted a tractor approaching the pothole where he sat. Without another thought, the four-legged creature jumped from the pothole to safety.

Later that day, his animal friends crossed his path. "How did you get free?" they asked. "We thought you couldn't get out."

"Oh, I couldn't," responded the turtle, "but then I saw a farmer on his tractor approaching, and I had to get out."

According to psychologist Rollo May, we choose not to change—or get out of life's potholes—until we hurt intensely enough. Maybe there is a lesson to be learned from this fictional account.

Glenn Van Ekeren
The Speaker's Sourcebook

Have you ever waited to do something you knew you had to do—because it was just too *painful*?

_____

What were the circumstances that finally made you do what you were *avoiding*?

_____

_____

_____

_____

_____

_____

_____

_____

_____

_____

_____

_____

_____

*In the end we will conserve only what we love.
We will love only what we understand. We will
understand only what we are taught.*

                                        Senegalese Saying

What does this quote mean to you?

_____

_____

_____

_____

_____

_____

_____

_____

_____

_____

_____

_____

_____

_____

_____

_____

_____

Not everything that is faced can be changed. But nothing can be changed until it is faced.

James Baldwin

Are there things about yourself that you are unable to face?

_____

_____

On this page or on a separate sheet of paper, write down the things you have trouble facing.

_____

_____

_____

_____

_____

_____

_____

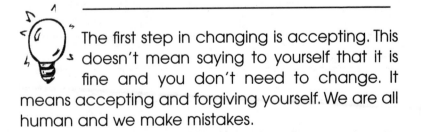

The first step in changing is accepting. This doesn't mean saying to yourself that it is fine and you don't need to change. It means accepting and forgiving yourself. We are all human and we make mistakes.

I'm learning more and more that love __plus__ attachment equals pain.

Lisa Bonet

What does this quote mean to you?

_____

_____

_____

Have you ever been too attached to someone?

_____

_____

What happened?

_____

_____

_____

_____

_____

What did you learn?

_____

_____

_____

_____

I've learned that nobody's perfect, and I don't expect myself to be perfect anymore.

Carly Simon

Have you learned that nobody's perfect?

_____

_____

Do you expect yourself to be perfect?

_____

_____

What imperfections about yourself do you accept?

_____

_____

_____

_____

_____

_____

_____

_____

_____

Have you ever been in a situation where you felt totally different about something than your friend did?

_____

_____

Were you able to see both sides?

_____

_____

_____

_____

_____

_____

Do you try to always look at both sides of a situation?

_____

_____

_____

_____

_____

_____

_____

_____

Our prime purpose in this life is to help others.
And if you can't help them at least don't hurt them.

The Dalai Lama

Write about a time you remember when you hurt someone.

_____

_____

_____

_____

_____

_____

_____

_____

How did you feel?

_____

_____

_____

_____

 _____

_____

_____

Could you have done anything differently?

_____

_____

_____

_____

_____

_____

_____

_____

What did you learn ?

_____

_____

_____

_____

_____

_____

_____

_____

_____

_____

Use the following pages to write about learning lessons. You can come back to these pages when you want to remember the lesson you learned or how you felt about a particular situation.

Lessons

Lessons

Lessons

_____

_____

_____

_____

_____

_____

_____

_____

_____

_____

_____

_____

_____

_____

_____

_____

_____

_____

_____

_____

_____

_____

Lessons

Lessons

_____

_____

_____

_____

_____

_____

_____

_____

_____

_____

_____

_____

_____

_____

_____

_____

_____

_____

_____

_____

_____

_____

Lessons

Lessons

_____

_____

_____

_____

_____

_____

_____

_____

_____

_____

_____

_____

_____

_____

_____

_____

_____

_____

_____

_____

Lessons

_____

_____

_____

_____

_____

_____

_____

_____

_____

_____

_____

_____

_____

_____

_____

_____

_____

_____

_____

_____

Lessons

Follow Your Dreams

8.

Follow Your Dreams

Strive hard. . . . .

Let your heart be your guide. . . . .

Hold fast to dreams,
for if dreams die
life is a broken winged
bird that cannot fly.
Hold fast to dreams,
for when dreams go,
life is a barren field
frozen with snow.

Langston Hughes

Follow Your Dreams

What are your dreams? Have you thought about what you want to do, where you want to be ten, twenty years from now? There are many professionals who would say that being specific about your goals is the number-one key to reaching them.

In this chapter, we are going to look at your dreams and goals. There will be questions that will help you clarify what you want to do, and there will be ample opportunity to look closely at what is standing in your way. Use this chapter, let it help you become clear about your hopes and dreams. Being able to make a living doing what makes you happy is probably the best situation you could hope for. We believe that no matter who you are, where you come from, or what it is that you want to do, it is possible. It isn't easy, but it is possible. Throughout the chapter, we will give you examples of people who have lived their dreams and overcome great obstacles to do so. There is no reason whatsoever why you cannot add your name to that list. (Remember, the more unlikely it seems now, the better story it will make later.)

Follow your bliss.

Joseph Campbell

What does this quote mean?

_____

_____

_____

_____

What is your bliss?

_____

_____

Do you have a dream?

_____

_____

What is your number-one goal?

_____

_____

_____

Do you believe dreams can come true?

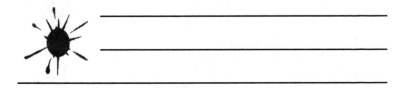

_____

_____

_____

What do you want to do for a living?

_____

_____

_____

_____

Do you believe the quote that says, "Do what you love and the money will follow"?

_____

_____

_____

_____

Do you believe your dreams will come true?

_____

_____

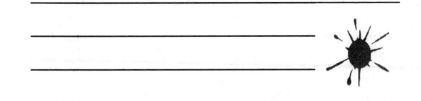

_____

_____

SOME THINGS TO THINK ABOUT

- Walt Disney was fired by a newspaper editor for lack of ideas. He also went bankrupt several times before he built Disneyland.
- Albert Einstein did not speak until he was four years old and didn't read until he was seven. His teacher described him as "mentally slow, unsociable and adrift forever in his foolish dreams." He was expelled from school.
- Leo Tolstoy, author of *War and Peace*, flunked out of college. He was described as "both unable and unwilling to learn."
- Abraham Lincoln ran for public office seven times and was defeated every time before becoming president of the United States.
- Beethoven was told at an early age that he had no talent for music.
- John Lennon was labeled, "learning disabled."

- Michael Jordan was cut from his high school basketball team.
- The Beatles were turned down by Decca Recording Company because "Groups of guitars are on their way out."
- When Lucille Ball began studying to become an actress in 1927, she was told by the head instructor of the John Murray Anderson Drama School, "Try another profession. Any other."
- Leon Uris, author of the bestseller *Exodus*, failed high school English three times.
- Woody Allen flunked motion picture production at New York University and the City College of New York. He also failed English at N.Y.U.
- Marilyn Monroe, when inquiring about modeling work, was told, "You better learn secretarial work or else get married."

Jack Canfield and Mark Victor Hansen

If you were _guaranteed_ that _whatever_ your dream for your future was you _could_ achieve it, what would it be?

_____

_____

_____

_____

_____

_____

_____

_____

_____

_____

Would your answer be different if you didn't have the guarantee?

_____

_____

_____

_____

_____

How Wrong You Were, Mr. Wright

In 1870, a shortsighted bishop expressed to the president of a small college his firm conviction that nothing new could be invented. The educator responded in disagreement and believed there was much yet to be discovered.

"Why, I believe it may even be possible for men in the future to fly through the air like birds," the college president said.

The bishop was taken aback. "Flying is reserved for the angels," he insisted. "I beg you not to mention that again lest you be guilty of blasphemy!"

That mistaken bishop was none other than Milton Wright, the father of Orville and Wilbur. Only thirty-three years later, his two sons made their first flight in a heavier-than-air machine, which was the forerunner of the airplane. How wrong you were, Mr. Wright!

Glenn Van Ekeren
The Speaker's Sourcebook

Do you have a dream that is far-fetched?

_____

_____

Are you going to pursue it anyway?

_____

Make a list of the things that you believe might prevent you from achieving your goals.

_____

_____

_____

_____

_____

_____

_____

_____

_____

_____

_____

_____

_____

_____

_____

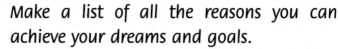

Your chances of success in any undertaking can always be measured by your belief in yourself.

Robert Collier

Do you believe in yourself?

_____

Make a list of all the reasons you can achieve your dreams and goals.

_____

_____

_____

_____

_____

_____

_____

_____

_____

_____

_____

It's an Uphill Climb

Paul Harvey has said, "You can tell when you are on the road to success. It's uphill all the way."

A young man in Kansas City, with a burning desire to draw, understood the uphill climb to success. He went from newspaper to newspaper trying to sell his cartoons. But each editor coldly and quickly suggested that he had no talent and implied that he might want to choose another line of work. But he persevered, determined to make his dream a reality. He wanted to draw, and draw he would.

For several months, the rejections came. Finally, in a move of "grace," he was hired by a minister to draw pictures advertising church events. This young artist was not discouraged by his unusual opportunity. Rather, he remembered the wise words of Benjamin Disraeli: "The secret of success in life is for a man to be ready for his opportunity when it comes."

Working out of a small, mouse-infested shed owned by the church, he struggled to be creative. Ironically, this less-than-ideal working environment stimulated his most famous work. He called it Mickey Mouse. And, of course, the man about whom we are talking was Walt Disney.

Walt Disney made it happen because he realized the uphill climb to success contained the opportunities on which he would capitalize.

Glenn Van Ekeren
The Speaker's Sourcebook

To accomplish great things, we must not only act but also dream, not only dream but also believe.

Anatole France

Write a story about yourself. Have the story take place in the future and have yourself living your dreams. Once you get started, see where it goes without "thinking" about it too much.

_____

_____

_____

_____

_____

_____

_____

_____

_____

_____

_____

_____

_____

My Future Story . . . (continued)

_____

_____

_____

_____

_____

_____

_____

_____

_____

_____

_____

_____

_____

_____

_____

_____

_____

Use the following pages to write about your dreams. You may have many dreams and your dreams may change. It doesn't matter—write them all down. Ten years from now, it will be fun to read this chapter and see how many of your dreams came true.

You are never given a wish
without also being given the power to make it true.

Richard Bach

_____

_____

_____

_____

_____

_____

_____

_____

_____

_____

Follow
Your dreams _____

Follow
Your dreams

Follow Your dreams

Follow
Your dreams

Follow
Your dreams

Follow Your dreams

Follow
Your dreams

Follow
Your dreams

Follow
Your dreams

Not in Vain

If I can stop one heart from breaking
I shall not live in vain;
If I can ease one life
from aching,
Or cool one pain,
Or help one fainting robin
Into his nest again,
I shall not live in vain.

Emily Dickinson

MAKING A DIFFERENCE

There is no question that we all want to make a difference. It is a natural human desire to want to know that your contributions have resulted in something or someone being better off. It makes us happy to make a difference, whether it be a party that you made better by telling jokes, a school project that was more interesting due to your input, or a nursing home that now has happier patients as a result of your volunteering. At the end of the day, if we feel that we have made a difference in the lives of others then we feel that our life has meaning.

There are many schools that are now participating in programs where the students earn credit for community service. This is the kind of program where everyone involved benefits: what we call a win/win situation. If your school is not yet participating, you might want to suggest it to your principal. The teenagers that we have spoken to who have this program at their school thoroughly enjoy it.

In this chapter, we will look at the things we do to make a difference, and will get in touch with how little it takes to brighten up someone else's day. You will have an opportunity to write about the things you have done and what others have done for you that have made a difference.

We invite you to write to us with ideas of things that teenagers can do to "Make a Difference." We will post your ideas on the <u>Chicken Soup for the Teenage Soul</u> Web page (<u>www.teenagechickensoup.com</u>).

ONE AT A TIME

A friend of ours was walking down a deserted Mexican beach at sunset. As he walked along, he began to see another man in the distance. As he grew nearer, he noticed that the local native kept leaning down, picking something up and throwing it out into the water. Time and again he kept hurling things out into the ocean.

As our friend approached even closer, he noticed that the man was picking up starfish that had been washed up on the beach and, one at a time, he was throwing them back into the water.

Our friend was puzzled. He approached the man and said, "Good evening, friend. I was wondering what you are doing."

"I'm throwing these starfish back into the ocean. You see, it's low tide right now and all of these starfish have been washed up onto the shore. If I don't throw them back into the sea, they'll die up here from the lack of oxygen."

"I understand," my friend replied, "but there must be thousands of starfish on this beach. You can't possibly get to all of them. There are simply too many. And don't you realize this is probably happening on hundreds of beaches all up and down this coast? Can't you see that you can't possibly make a difference?"

The local native smiled, bent down and picked up yet another starfish, and as he threw it back into the sea, he replied, "Made a difference to that one!"

Jack Canfield and Mark Victor Hansen

We may feel that what we can do to make a difference is too small and insignificant, but if we all would do something, think of how much of a difference that would make.

What would you like to do to make a difference?

_____

_____

_____

_____

_____

_____

_____

_____

_____

_____

_____

_____

_____

_____

What have you done to make a difference?

_____

_____

_____

_____

_____

_____

_____

_____

Give an example of something you did for others that in turn affected you.

_____

_____

_____

_____

_____

_____

_____

WHY ARE WE HERE?

Albert Einstein reflected on the purpose of man's existence when he said, "Strange is our situation here upon earth. Each of us comes for a short visit, not knowing why, yet sometimes seeming to a divine purpose. From the standpoint of daily life, however, there is one thing we do know: That we are here for the sake of others . . . for the countless unknown souls with whose fate we are connected by a bond of sympathy. Many times a day, I realize how much my own outer and inner life is built upon the labors of people, both living and dead, and how earnestly I must exert myself in order to give in return as much as I have received."

Glenn Van Ekeren
<u>The Speaker's Sourcebook</u>

Do you agree with this?

_____

What things do you enjoy that are due to the efforts of others? (e.g., running water, television, freedom).

_____

_____

_____

_____

_____

What would you like to give in return? (Use the following pages to write about all the ways in which you want to make a difference.)

_____

_____

_____

_____

_____

_____

_____

_____

_____

_____

_____

_____

_____

_____

_____

_____

_____

_____

_____

_____

Making
a Difference

Making a Difference

Making a Difference

Making
a Difference

Making
a Difference

Making a Difference

Making
a Difference

Making a Difference

_____

_____

_____

_____

_____

_____

_____

_____

_____

_____

_____

_____

_____

_____

_____

_____

_____

_____

_____

_____

_____

_____

10.

Growing Up

Relax, you're on a journey of discovery. Let life reveal itself to you.

Melodie Beattie

GROWING UP

The sound of those two words together sparks all kinds of reactions and images in our minds. "Grow up!" "No, you're not grown up enough to do that!" "Only grown-ups can go there." "Oh my, look at how grown-up you are." "Why don't you just grow up already?"... and on and on.

Sometimes you probably feel like you are being pulled in two different directions, and you know what? You are!

The teenage years are transition years. You are changing from a child to an adult. You are drawn to more grown-up activities, and yet you yearn to play like a child with total abandon. The answer is to feel comfortable with both. You will grow up. Nature is at work here, and you are along for the ride.

You are beginning to break away from some of your deeper ties to your parents. You are dealing with problems that a year ago you didn't know how to pronounce. You are beginning to worry about things that used to be only your parents' concerns. You can't wait to leave home and yet the idea terrifies you. You are developing your own opinions and feelings about things and more often than not, they are different from your parents' thoughts and feelings. All this is nature's way of making you an independent human being.

The difficulties that you are experiencing—the pushing and pulling, the constant fighting (both internal and external)—is just the transitory madness. **It won't always be like this.**

Try to imagine you are on a ride. The ups and downs and all the other craziness are simply part of the ride. There are things to let go of and things to grab hold of. The ride is going very fast, but don't resist it. Relax, breathe and enjoy. There is nothing to be scared of—in fact, it is pretty exciting. You are growing up!

The big question is whether you are going to be able to say a big hearty yes to your adventure.

Joseph Campbell

How old are you? _____

How old do you feel? _____

What do you think is the perfect age? _____

What would you like to do with your life? _____

_____

_____

How old do you think people should be before they :

Get a job_____

Cook for themselves _____

Set their own bedtimes _____

Go away with friends_____

Do their own laundry _____

Have a boyfriend or girlfriend_____

Date_____

Kiss _____

Stay out past midnight_____

Stay out as late as they want _____

Have their own phones _____

Drive _____

Travel alone _____

Drink _____

Go to clubs _____

Get married _____

Have children _____

Vote _____

Go out by themselves _____

What other things do you think people should be of a certain age to do?

_____

_____

_____

_____

_____

_____

_____

_____

_____

_____

LIFE

Oh how our lives have been planned out,
Until eighteen without a doubt.
School, college, clubs and games,
Long-standing traditions, pre-given names.
Identity given and taken away,
Being yourself at the end of the day.
Parents, teachers, sisters and brothers,
All caring for you, like most others.
Degrees, qualifications, aims and traditions,
Trying to fulfil dreams and ambitions.
Constant reminders of glory to come,
We will touch others, i.e., only some.
Remember your success is all up to you
It's all yours, what will you do?

Gemma Hobcraft

It may be all right to be content with what you have; never with what you are.

B. C. Forbes

At what age do you think a person is mature? _____

Do you think maturity is a good thing? _____

Do you think all adults are mature? _____

Do you think a difficult life makes a person grow up faster?

_____

Describe "grown-up."

_____

_____

_____

_____

_____

_____

_____

_____

_____

_____

LIMBO

I see myself on a hill of green
Against a backdrop of the deepest blue,
Speckled with bursts of light called stars—
This is the sanctuary of which I knew.
Not yet an adult I sit here confined,
In a room in my mother's house.
I want so much the taste of freedom,
But my endeavors are promptly doused.
People leave me, grown up, to the world,
A baby in the cradle, I'm left behind.
All that's left are pictures and memories
Slowly drifting out of mind.
Responsibilities are growing with importance,
Time is growing short each passing of the light,
I'm gradually climbing toward adulthood,
Into the mist of an uncertain night.
The universe seems a bit more out of reach,
And not as friendly as I once thought.
I'm being pushed to a corner of my own,
The rosy glasses have been, finally, taken off.
Enthusiasm to achieve is loud and strong,
The need to break free is overwhelming,
Yet the chains that link me home
Are ever taut and binding,
For I'm too young, and yet too old,
An awkward sense of loss.
Where shall I go, what shall I be,
And who will pay the cost?
I cannot trouble myself with these thoughts,
Which I'll ponder throughout time,
So I must live and laugh and love,
And pray to keep my mind.

Natalia Sorman

Can you relate to the poem "Limbo"?

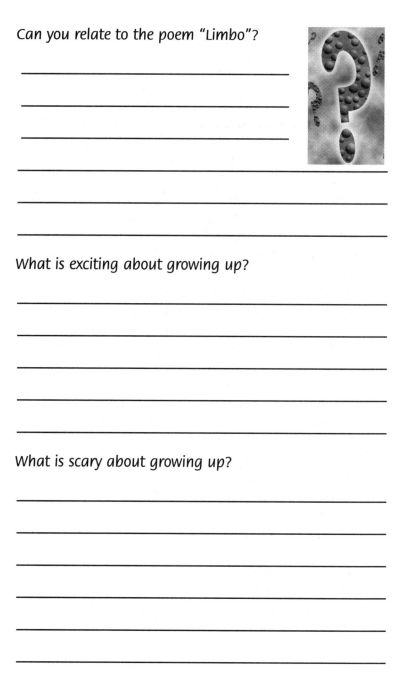

_____

_____

_____

_____

_____

_____

What is exciting about growing up?

_____

_____

_____

_____

_____

What is scary about growing up?

_____

_____

_____

_____

_____

_____

_____

Describe a situation in which you felt your actions were very grown-up.

_____

_____

_____

_____

_____

_____

_____

Describe a situation in which you felt your actions were very immature.

_____

_____

_____

_____

_____

_____

_____

_____

_____

Does your family treat you like a grown-up?

_____

_____

_____

_____

_____

_____

_____

Describe what that is like.

_____

_____

_____

_____

_____

_____

_____

_____

Do you think of yourself as grown-up?

_____

_____

_____

_____

Do you want to be considered grown-up?

_____

_____

_____

_____

Who treats you the most like a grown-up?

_____

_____

_____

_____

What does that feel like?

_____

_____

_____

_____

LOOK INSIDE FOR HAPPINESS

There is an ancient Native American legend about a little-known tribe that was constantly at war with other Native American tribes. They abused their religion and their families, had no morals or feelings for others, laughed at wisdom or any kind of order. Murder, rape, theft and plundering were daily occurrences. This violent tribe seemed doomed to wipe themselves off the face of the earth.

Finally, an old chief gathered together a few of the least violent braves and held a council to discuss how they could save their tribe from themselves. The wise old chief decided the only thing to do was to take the secret of happiness and success away from those who abused it. They would take this secret and hide it where no one would ever find it again. The big question was—where should they hide it?

One brave suggested they bury the secret of happiness and success deep in the earth. But the chief said, "No, that will never do, for man will dig deep down into the earth and find it."

Another brave said to sink the secret into the dark depths of the deepest ocean. But again the chief replied, "No, not there, for man will learn to dive into the dark depths of the ocean and will find it."

A third brave thought they should take it to the top of the highest mountain and hide it there. But again, the chief said, "No, for man will eventually climb even the highest of mountains and find it, and again take it up for himself."

Finally, the old chief had the answer. "Here is what we will do with the secret of happiness and success," he stated. "We will hide it deep inside of man himself, for he will never think to look for it there."

To this day, according to that old Native American legend, man has been running to and fro all over the earth—digging, diving and climbing—searching for something that he already possesses within himself.

Glenn Van Ekeren
The Speaker's Sourcebook

Are you happy?

_____

_____

What do you think is the secret to happiness?

_____

_____

_____

_____

_____

_____

_____

_____

_____

_____

_____

_____

_____

_____

_____

Think for a minute about yourself and where you are right now.

Then think about where you want to go with your life . . . what you want to do and be, etc. Think about all the obstacles you might face. Think about what inner strengths and qualities you will need to be able to overcome those obstacles.

We have given you many pages for this because this is a great way to make a positive impact on your future—now.

Growing Up

_____

_____

_____

_____

_____

_____

_____

_____

_____

_____

_____

_____

_____

_____

_____

_____

_____

_____

_____

_____

_____

Growing Up

_____

_____

_____

_____

_____

_____

_____

_____

_____

_____

_____

_____

_____

_____

_____

_____

_____

_____

_____

_____

Growing Up

Growing Up

_____

_____

_____

_____

_____

_____

_____

_____

_____

_____

_____

_____

_____

_____

_____

_____

_____

_____

_____

_____

_____

_____

_____

Growing Up

_____

_____

Growing Up

_____

_____

_____

_____

_____

_____

_____

_____

_____

_____

_____

_____

_____

_____

_____

_____

_____

_____

_____

_____

_____

_____

_____

_____

_____

_____

_____

Growing Up

_____

_____

_____

_____

_____

_____

_____

_____

_____

_____

_____

_____

_____

_____

_____

_____

_____

_____

_____

_____

_____

Growing Up

AFTERWORD

What we call the beginning is often the end. And to make an end is to make a beginning. The end is where we start from.

T. S. Eliot

Well . . . here we are at the end of the journal. Of course, as Mr. Eliot has said so beautifully, the end is only a new beginning. Wise words to remember as you go through so many changes. When a relationship ends, it is just making way for a new one. When a friendship falls apart because one or both of you has changed "too much," remember the "change" made you ready for another friendship. And as some of you prepare to leave for college or move away from home to begin a career, the closeness you have with your parents will turn into a new kind of closeness.

We hope that these pages have helped you, guided you and motivated you to explore your life. We hope that this journal has served you, supported you, and, most of all, helped you to see you are not alone on this journey.

When you have completed this journal, we know it will become one of your most valued possessions. Hold onto it, store it safely away and return to it from time to time. Maybe someday you will read it again, when your children are teens and you want to remember the "way it was."

We love you and thank you for letting us be a part of your process. Please write to us and tell us how this journal has affected you and share with us any feedback you have.

Also, if you would like to submit any stories or poems that you wrote in here, please do.

Send your story to:
Chicken Soup for the Teenage Soul
P.O. Box 936
Pacific Palisades, CA 90272
e-mail **stories only** to:
stories@teenagechickensoup.com
e-mail **letters only** to:
letters@teenagechickensoup.com
fax: 310-573-3657
Web site: *www.teenagechickensoup.com*

If you would like a return response to your letter or submission, please enclose a self-addressed stamped envelope.

<u>MORE CHICKEN SOUP?</u>

Many of the stories and poems you read in this journal were submitted by readers like you. We are currently working on more *Chicken Soup for the Teenage Soul* books.

We would love to have you contribute a story, poem, cartoon or suggestion for any of these future books. This may be a story you write yourself, or one you clip out of the school newspaper, local newspaper, a church bulletin, or a magazine. It might be something you read in a book or find on the Internet. It could also be a favorite poem, quotation, or cartoon you have saved. Please also send us as much information as possible about where it came from.

Kimberly would love to hear any suggestions you have regarding the issues you think should be covered in future books, or any questions you would like to ask that may be included in the book.

Just send a copy of your stories or other pieces to us at this address:

Chicken Soup for the Teenage Soul
P.O. Box 936
Pacific Palisades, CA 90272
e-mail **stories only** to:
stories@teenagechickensoup.com
e-mail **letters only** to:
letters@teenagechickensoup.com
fax: 310-573-3657
Web site: *www.teenagechickensoup.com*

WHAT IS A *CHICKEN SOUP* STORY?

After the release of *Chicken Soup for the Teenage Soul* in May 1997, we received close to twenty thousand submissions from teenagers for the second edition. We were amazed, to say the least, at how many of you wanted to share your wisdom and experience with other teens in hopes of helping them. Although every story was an inspiration, we often chose the one that was written more in the format of what we call "a *Chicken Soup* story."

In order to help you recognize and/or write one, we thought it would be helpful to describe to you what it is we look for in a story.

One of the most common mistakes in deciding what to write about is thinking it must be about something tragic. Since we felt deep and profound emotion when someone we loved died or became ill, we think that a story about it will move the reader in the same way. Although there are rare cases where this works, it usually does not. It is too personal and not interesting to the person reading it. Avoid eulogy-type stories.

Many people write to us with tributes to a friend or relative. Once again, this is something YOU feel strongly about. It is a good idea, before you write a story, to think to yourself: *If I did not know this person or have any emotions tied to the subject, would I be interested in the story?* If the answer is no, move on to another idea.

Another common mistake is vagueness. Someone once said, "God is in the details" and nothing could be more true when it comes to writing. Here is an example:

My boyfriend was so perfect. He was all I ever dreamed of and he was very nice to me. This is pretty vague.

The boy who I was in love with at the time was six feet tall, had a swimmer's body and the most stunning blue eyes I'd ever seen. On our first date he offered to take me home early because he knew I had to take my SATs the following morning. This is not vague. Which one is more interesting?

Whenever possible, write as if you are explaining what a camera would see, rather than what you are thinking.

A great *Chicken Soup* story has a great ending. A perfect example is the first story in *Chicken Soup for the Teenage Soul II*, called "Starlight, Star Bright." The author of this story doesn't let us know what the end is going to be until the very end. It feels like he might be laughing at her, (the author) or too embarrassed by her kiss, so, as the reader, you feel a bit nervous about the outcome. When you read the final sentence you are so relieved and so happy, it is as if *you* were the one he wanted to kiss. That is a good ending.

The most important thing about writing a story is knowing before you begin what the beginning, middle and end of the story will be. Change it around and play with it until you have the best possible ending. Once you know how the story will end you can build up to it. You can do that either by keeping the reader in suspense or by ending it with the wisdom you gained from the experience.

It is a great idea to go through this book, or the orginal **Chicken Soup for the Teenage Soul**, and read the endings of lots of different stories before you begin so you can get the hang of it.

Once you have followed these guidelines, let the rest happen from your heart.

The idea is to pass on wisdom and hope to the reader, leaving him with goosebumps and an open heart. That is what a *Chicken Soup* story is all about.

Good luck and have fun.

SUPPORTING TEENAGERS

In the spirit of supporting teenagers everywhere, we have formed T.E.E.N. (Teen Empowerment and Educational Network). A portion of the profits that are generated from this book will go to this network, which, in turn will support various teen organizations that are working toward the empowerment of teenagers and the improvement of teen education. Some organizations that will be receiving support from this network are:

Yellow Ribbon Project
Dyslexia Awareness and Resource Center
Teen Letter Project

The **Yellow Ribbon Project** is a nonprofit organization that helps to prevent teen suicides.

Since its story first appeared in *A 3rd Serving of Chicken Soup for the Soul* and then again in *Chicken Soup for the Teenage Soul*, Yellow Ribbon has documented over 1,000 lives saved. We were deeply moved by Dale and Dar Emme's dedication to preventing teen suicide because it came as a result of their losing their son to suicide. They have made hundreds of appearances at high schools and youth groups to discuss with teenagers this tragic epidemic and have marked results with each appearance.

Sharing & giving

To contact this organization for help in setting up a Yellow Ribbon Program in your school or community, or to receive a yellow ribbon for yourself and your friends:

Yellow Ribbon Project
P.O. Box 644 • Westminster, CO 80030
phone: 303-429-3530, -3531, -3532
fax: 303-426-4496
e-mail: *light4life@yellowribbon.org*
Web site: *www.yellowribbon.org*

The **Dyslexia Awareness and Resource Center** is an organization that helps students who are dyslexic learn how to read and learn in a way that is conducive to their disabilty. Research has shown that a large percentage of juveniles who are in prison or detention centers are dyslexic. Joan Esposito, program director for the Center, believes that because learning is so difficult for dyslexics, their self-esteem is continually damaged in our present educational system and this results in many teen dyslexics turning to crime.

We feel that the Center is doing very important work to reverse the effects of and prevent this disabling progression of circumstances and urge all those interested in doing similar work in their communities to contact the Center.

Sharing & giving

If you would like more information or if you are interested in making a donation please contact:

Dyslexia Awareness and Resource Center
928 Carpinteria Street, Suite 2
Santa Barbara, CA 93103
phone: 805-963-7339
fax: 805-963-6581
e-mail: *darc@silcom.com*
Web site: *http://www.dyslexia-center.com*

The **Teen Letter Project** is responsible for answering the heartfelt letters received from teenagers and also for reaching out to teens in trouble and encouraging them to seek professional help. The Project was founded by Kimberly Kirberger, along with Jack Canfield, Mark Victor Hansen and Health Communications, Inc.

The Project is currently involved in setting up a Web page that will allow teens to give help to and receive help from one another.

To contact the Teen Letter Project:

Teen Letter Project
P. O. Box 936
Pacific Palisades, CA 90272
phone: 310-573-3655
fax: 510-573-3657
e-mail for stories: *stories@teenagechickensoup.com*
e-mail for letters: *letters@teenagechickensoup.com*
Web site: *www.teenagechickensoup.com*

TEEN HELP HOTLINES

Al-Anon/Al-A-Teen • 800-344-2666

Center for Substance Abuse Treatment • 800-662-HELP

Children of the Night Hotline • 800-551-1300

Gang Hotline • 800-900-GANG

Gay & Lesbian Youth Line • 800-347-TEEN

National AIDS Hotline • 800-342-2437

National Child Abuse Hotline • 800-422-4453

National Runaway Switchboard • 800-621-4000

Nine Line (teens in crisis with families or in schools)
800-999-9999

Teen AIDS Hotline • 800-234-TEEN

Youth Crisis Hotline • 800-448-4663

SUGGESTED READING

Angelou, Maya. *The Complete Collected Poems of Maya Angelou.* New York: Random House, 1994.

Colgrove, Melba. *How to Survive the Loss of a Love.* Los Angeles: Prelude Press, 1993.

Gardner, Richard A. *The Boys & Girls Book About Divorce.* New York: Bantam, 1985.

James, Jennifer. *Women & the Blues: Passions That Hurt, Passions That Heal.* San Francisco: HarperSan Francisco, 1990.

Jampolsky, Gerald G. *Good-Bye to Guilt.* New York: Bantam, 1985.

Kübler-Ross, Elisabeth. *On Death and Dying.* Indianapolis, Ind.: Macmillan, 1991.

LeShan, Eda. *Learning to Say Good-Bye: When a Child's Parent Dies.* New York: Avon, 1978.

Pipher, Mary. *Reviving Ophelia: Saving the Selves of Adolescent Girls.* New York: Putnam Publishing Group, 1994.

Shiras, Frank. *Go Ask Alice.* Woodstock, N.Y.: The Dramatic Publishing Co., 1976.

WHO IS JACK CANFIELD?

Jack Canfield is a bestselling author and one of America's leading experts in the development of human potential. He is both a dynamic and entertaining speaker and a highly sought-after trainer with a wonderful ability to inform and inspire audiences to open their hearts, love more openly and boldly pursue their dreams.

Jack spent his teenage years growing up in Martins Ferry, Ohio, and Wheeling, West Virginia, with his sister, Kimberly (Kirberger), and his two brothers, Rick and Taylor. The whole family has spent most of their professional careers dedicated to educating, counseling and empowering teens—Rick is a psychotherapist in Phoenix, Arizona, who specialized in working with teens for many years, and Taylor is currently a special-education teacher working with teens in Tampa, Florida. Jack admits to being shy and lacking self-confidence in high school, but through a lot of hard work he managed to earn letters in three sports and graduate third in his class.

After graduating college Jack taught high school in the inner city of Chicago and in Iowa. Most of his professional career after that has been spent teaching teachers how to empower teenagers to believe in themselves and to go for their dreams. In recent years Jack has expanded this to include adults in both educational and corporate settings.

Sharing & giving

Sharing — giving

He is the author and narrator of several bestselling audio and videocassette programs, including *Self-Esteem and Peak Performance, How to Build High Self-Esteem* and *The GOALS Program.* He is a regularly consulted expert for radio and television broadcasts and has published twenty-five books—all bestsellers within their categories—including nineteen *Chicken Soup for the Soul* books, *The Aladdin Factor, Heart at Work, 100 Ways to Build Self-Concept in the Classroom,* and *Dare to Win.*

Jack addresses over 100 groups each year. His clients include professional associations, school districts, government agencies, churches and corporations. His clients have also included schools and school districts in all fifty states; over 100 education associations, including the American School Counselors Association, the California Peer Counselors Association, and Californians for a Drug Free Youth; plus corporate clients such as AT&T, Campbell Soup, Clairol, Domino's Pizza, G.E., New England Telephone, Re/Max, Sunkist, Supercuts and Virgin Records.

Jack conducts an annual eight-day Training of Trainers program in the areas of building self-esteem and achieving peak performance. It attracts educators, counselors, parenting trainers, corporate trainers, professional speakers, ministers and others interested in developing their speaking and seminar-leading skills in these areas.

For further information about Jack's books, tapes and trainings, or to schedule him for a presentation, please contact:

The Canfield Training Group

P.O. Box 30880 • Santa Barbara , CA 93130
phone: 800-237-8336 • fax: 805-563-2945
e-mail: *speaking@canfieldgroup.com*
Web site: *www.chickensoup.com*

WHO IS MARK VICTOR HANSEN?

Mark Victor Hansen is a professional speaker who, in the last twenty years, has made over four thousand presentations to more than 2 million people in thirty-three countries. His presentations cover sales excellence and strategies; personal empowerment and development; and how to triple your income and double your time off.

Mark has spent a lifetime dedicated to his mission of making a profound and positive difference in people's lives. Throughout his career, he has inspired hundreds of thousands of people to create a more powerful and purposeful future for themselves while stimulating the sale of billions of dollars worth of goods and services.

Mark is a prolific writer and has authored *Future Diary, How to Achieve Total Prosperity* and *The Miracle of Tithing.* He is the coauthor of the *Chicken Soup for the Soul* series, *Dare to Win* and *The Aladdin Factor* (all with Jack Canfield) and *The Master Motivator* (with Joe Batten).

Mark has also produced a complete library of personal empowerment audio- and videocassette programs that have enabled his listeners to recognize and better use their innate abilities in their business and personal lives. His message has made him a popular television and radio personality, with appearances on ABC, NBC, CBS, HBO, PBS, QVC and CNN.

He has also appeared on the cover of numerous magazines, including *Success*, *Entrepreneur* and *Changes*.

Mark is a big man with a heart and a spirit to match—an inspiration to all who seek to better themselves.

For further information about Mark, contact:

Mark Victor Hansen & Associates
P.O. Box 7665 • Newport Beach, CA 92658
phone: 949-759-9304 or 800-433-2314
fax: 949-722-6912
Web site: *www.chickensoup.com*

WHO IS KIMBERLY KIRBERGER?

Kimberly Kirberger is the president and founder of I.A.M. for Teens, Inc. (Inspiration and Motivation for Teens, Inc.) a corporation formed exclusively to work *for* teens. It is her goal to see teens represented in a more positive light and it is her strong belief that teens deserve better and more positive treatment.

She spends her time reading the thousands of letters and stories sent to her by teen readers and traveling around the country speaking to high school students and parents of teens. She has appeared as a teen expert on many television and radio shows, including *Geraldo, MSNBC,* and *The Terry Bradshaw Show.*

Kimberly is the coauthor of the bestselling *Chicken Soup for the Teenage Soul,* as well as *Chicken Soup for the Teenage Soul II.* She worked closely with teenagers on both projects and feels her ability to listen to their needs and wants lent to the success of the teenage *Chicken Soup* books.

She started the Teen Letter Project with Jack Canfield, Mark Victor Hansen and Health Communications, Inc. The Project is responsible for answering the heartfelt letters received from teenagers and also reaching out to teens in trouble and encouraging them to seek professional help.

The Teen Letter Project is currently involved in setting up a Web page that will allow teens to give help to and receive help from one another.

Kimberly is also the coauthor of the forthcoming *Chicken Soup for the College Soul, Chicken Soup for the Parent's Soul, Chicken Soup for the Teenage Soul III* and a book about relationships for teenagers.

To book Kimberly for a speaking engagement, or for further information on any of her projects, please contact:

I.A.M. for Teens, Inc.
P.O. Box 936 • Pacific Palisades, CA 90272
phone: 310-573-3655 • fax: 310-573-3657
Web site: *www.teenagechickensoup.com*

CONTRIBUTORS

Lissa Barker is a fifteen-year-old freshman in high school in Omaha, Nebraska. She is a cheerleader, as well as a member of the varsity track and cross-country teams, and of many clubs. Lissa enjoys spending time with her friends and family, running, shopping, and, of course, writing. After high school, she plans on attending Princeton University and going into politics.

Lyndsie Chlowitz is sixteen years old. She is a varsity cheerleader and is very much involved in her school. Lyndsie has a great love for dance as well as poetry. Her writing career began when she was in fourth grade, and she won a Los Angeles County essay contest.

Carrie Cohen is double majoring in psychology and English at Syracuse University. When she is not in the midst of a tragic relationship or protesting the injustices of a male-dominated patriarchal society, this caffeine fiend can usually be found driving around in her car, Lolita, or obsessively checking her e-mail. She can be reached by e-mail: *nccohen@mailbox.syr.edu.*

Lilian "Lica" Gamble recently graduated from Mount Carmel Academy in New Orleans, Louisiana and will be attending Millsaps College in the fall. She wrote this poem two years ago for a friend who grieved the loss of a friend to suicide. Lilian values all human life-born or unborn, known or unknown.

Randy Glasbergen is the creator of the cartoon *The Better Half,* which is syndicated to 150 newspapers by King Features Syndicate. More than twenty thousand of Randy's cartoons have been published in magazines, books and greeting cards around the world. Look for Randy's daily cartoons online @ *www.norwich.net/~randyg/toon.html.*

Gemma Hobcraft is fifteen years old and lives and works in England. According to her friends she is a great friend—someone who enjoys writing, is fun to be with and loves diving and drama. Her friends say, "Life wouldn't be the same without her and her zany sense of humor!"

Denise Marigold is an eighteen-year-old high school student. She plans to pursue a career in pediatric medicine, although she has always had a passion

for writing. The *Chicken Soup for the Soul* books have inspired and encouraged her to go for her dreams. She is honored to be included in this publication.

Kathryn Mockett is fourteen years old and lives Bedfordshire, England. She as a sixteen-year-old brother and a dog named Judy. She attends Berkhamsted Collegiate School in Hertfordshire and is currently studying the piano.

Jamie Newland is a fourteen-year-old student at Mason High School. Her life's dream is to be an actress and to continue writing as well—and, eventually, to have one of her novels published. Jamie has many things she wants to accomplish in her lifetime, yet above all she hopes that others will see her as a fair, hard-working, big dreaming Christian girl.

Peer Resources is a leading authority in peer helping services, programs, and resources for children, teens and adults. They can be contacted by e-mail at *helping@islandnet.com* or visited at *www.islandnet.com/~rcarr/peer.html*. Write to 1052 Davie St., Victoria, BC V8S 4E3 or call 800-567-3700.

Danielle Rosenblatt is a fourteen-year-old junior high school student who lives in Allentown, Pennsylvania. She plans to be an actress, a pediatrician, a lawyer or an elementary school teacher, and to publish a book someday. For now, she enjoys just being a teenager.

Harley Schwadron is a self-taught cartoonist living in Ann Arbor, Michigan and worked as a journalist and public relations writer before switching to cartooning full-time in 1984. His cartoons appear in *Barron's, Harvard Business Review, Wall Street Journal, National Law Journal* and many others. He can be reached at P.O. Box 1347, Ann Arbor, MI 48106 or by calling 313-426-8433.

Natalia Sorman was born in Bloomington, Illinois on December 8, 1980. Her parents divorced in 1984 and her father took off shortly thereafter. Natalia and her mom moved to Niles, Illinois in 1990. She just recently found her father in Chicago. Natalia is a junior at Maine Township High School East in Park Ridge, Illinois. She has been writing since she was twelve years old.

Tiffany Trutenko is currently a high school sophomore who lives near Chicago, Illinois. She enjoys cheerleading, playing soccer, talking on the phone and hanging out with her friends. She hopes to attend San Diego State University when she graduates from high school.

Glenn Van Ekeren is a dynamic professional speaker and trainer who is dedicated to helping people and organizations maximize their potential. Glenn is the author of *The Speaker's Sourcebook*, *The Speaker's Sourcebook II* and the popular *Potential* newsletter. Glenn has a variety of written publications and audio and video presentations available. He can be reached at People Building Institute, 330 Village Circle, Sheldon, IA 51201 or by calling 800-899-4878.

Khendi White was born in Gaithersburg, Maryland on December 6, 1985. She is a straight-A student currently in the seventh grade attending all honors classes at Earle B. Wood Middle School. She has been writing poetry since she was seven years old. Writing has always been her favorite hobby.

New for Little Souls

The New Kid and the Cookie Thief
Story adaptation by Lisa McCourt
Illustrated by Mary O'Keefe Young

For a shy girl like Julie, there couldn't be anything worse than the very first day at a brand new school. What if the kids don't like her? What if no one ever talks to her at all? Julie's big sister has some advice—and a plan—that just might help. But will Julie be too scared to even give it a try?

October 1998 Release • Code 5882, hardcover, $14.95

New for Kids

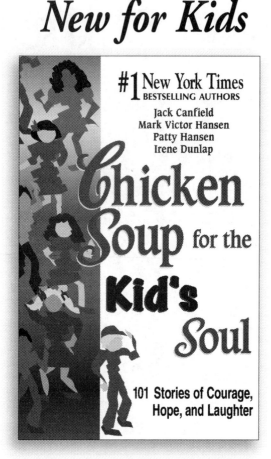

New for Teens

New York Times Bestseller!

Chicken Soup for the Teenage Soul

Jack Canfield, Mark Victor Hansen, and Kimberly Kirberger

This batch of *Chicken Soup* contains important lessons on the nature of friendship and love, the importance of belief in the future, the value of respect for oneself and others. Featuring contributions from stars Jennie Garth, Jennifer Love Hewitt, A.J. Langer and many more.
Code 4630, $12.95